Advanced praise for *Allure to the Undead*:

"Corvis Nocturnum continues to produce significant work on 'dark' subcultures from an emic perspective. *Allure of the Vampire* treats many artifacts of popular culture that have previously gone unanalyzed, offering a unique perspective into our fascination with the undead." ~ Joseph Laycock, author of *Vampires Today: The Truth about Modern Vampirism*

"*Allure of the Vampire* is not only a very entertaining retrospect of vampires in books, movies, music and other media, it allows you to form you own conclusions as to why there has been such a taboo desire--an insatiable lust--for wanting to know more about these dark, sensuous, dangerous creatures of lore. Such creatures have fascinated us, teased us, romanced us, scared us, and lured us into their forbidden domains for not years, but centuries--and will continue to do so for as long as they exist. If you enjoyed Corvis' *Embracing the Darkness*, you'll enjoy *Allure of the Vampire* just as much." ~ Cinsearae R. Santiago, Author: *ABRAXAS*, Editor/Publisher of *Dark Gothic Resurrected* magazine.

"As a writer and artist, Corvis Nocturnum guides us into the dark recesses of society with great insight and without judgment. This time he artfully digs even deeper, exploring our unceasing passion for the forbidden and specifically our undeniable attraction to Vampires: real, virtual, mythical, cinematic, or literary. In *Allure of the Vampire*, Corvis, once more, proves his mettle as the ultimate source for understanding real life darkness - those who inhabit the shadows and dark corners; those who happily fear them, those who love them; those who want to be love by them; . . . or be them. A definite MUST READ for all connoisseurs of the UNDEAD!" ~ Lenore, Founder of the Lost Children of the Oubliette

"*Allure of the Vampire* brings you a vision of vampires and sexuality in mythology, philosophy, literature, film and pop culture. It is always good to see Corvis Nocturnum making sincere efforts to bring a fresh view to the big picture of the vampire archetype." ~ Father Sebastiaan, author of the *Sanguinomicon* and Master Fangsmith of SABERTOOTH

"For even the most die hard vampire fan, there is bound to be something in this book you hadn't known about before." ~ Belinda, Lost Children of the Oubliette, Australian branc

Allure of the Vampire

Our Sexual Attraction to the Undead

By Corvis Nocturnum

Allure of the Vampire by Corvis Nocturnum

All rights reserved. No part of this book may be reproduced in part or whole in any format whatsoever without first contacting the author for permission.

ISBN: 1448658942

To contact the author, please refer to his official website:
www.corvisnocturnum.com

Or send an SASE to:
P.O. Box 11496, Fort Wayne, Indiana 46858-1496Other works by Corvis Nocturnum include:
Artwork inside of Julie Strain's Nightmare on Pinup Street (Heavy Metal, 2004) under the name of DarkartistV

Embracing the Darkness; Understanding Dark Subcultures, (Dark Moon, May 2005)

A Mirror Darkly, (Dark Moon Press, May 2006)

Promethean Flame, (Dark Moon Press, October 2008)

Allure of the Vampire by Corvis Nocturnum

TABLE OF CONTENTS

IMAGE CREDITS 1
ACKNOWLEDGMENTS 3
FOREWORD 5
INTRODUCTION 13
VAMPIRES IN FOLKLORE AND EARLY FICTION 18
    EARLY SUPERSTITIONS 20
        Other cultures 22
    THE DARK ROMANTICS 25
        Lord Byron 29
        Palidori 31
        Carmilla 32
        Bram Stoker 34
        Victorian times 36
        Alternative sexuality resurfaces 41
        Laurel K. Hamilton 44
        Twilight 47
        Romance novels 53
        Vampire Erotica 57
THE VAMPIRE ON THE SILVER SCREEN 60
        The Nude Vampire 64
        Hammer films 65
        Vampira 66
        Elvira, sex siren 67
        Red Vamp 69
        Lilith in film 72
        Barnabas Collins 75
        The Hunger 77
        Buffy 78
        Once Bitten 80
        Lost Boys 81
        Forever Knight 82
        The Vampire Chronicles 85
        Vampire in Brooklyn 88

    Embrace of the Vampire 88
    From Dusk Till Dawn 89
    Kindred: The Embraced 90
    John Carpenter's Vampires 92
    BloodRayne 93
    Van Helsing 94
    Underworld 94
    Vampire sexuality becomes overt 95
    The Insatiable 96
    Blood Ties 97
    True Blood 98
  PORNOGRAPHY AND THE VAMPIRE 103
    Dracula Sucks 103
    Les Vampyres 104

THE VAMPIRE IN ART 108

  PERFORMANCE ART 110
    Anders Manga 111
    Theatres Des Vampires 114
    Vlad and Sky 117
  VAMPIRES WALK AMONG US 119
    The Sci-Fi Channel 121
  THE VAMPIRE IN ART 124
    Vampirella 124
    Art of Tony Mauro 125
    Madame Webb Photography 126
    Vampire Wear 130
    Vampire Wine 132

VAMPIRE SEXUALIS 138

  PSYCHOLOGY OF THE VAMPIRE 140
    Jung's version of an archetype 142
    Crimes and deviant behavior 144
  REAL NIGHT STALKERS IN HISTORY 145
    Baron Gilles de Rais 147
    Bela Kiss 147
    Peter Kurten 149
    Psychopathia Sexualis 151
  MODERN CRIMINAL CASES 153
    Vampire Cults 153
    Rod Ferrell 157
    Clinical Vampirism 160
  MEDICAL CASES 160

> *Renfield's Syndrome* *161*
> VAMPIRES AND FETISH 166
> > *Blood fetishes* *167*

VAMPIRES OF OUR DAY 174
> THE GOOD, THE BAD AND THE ENERGY VAMPS 174
> VAMPIRES, BLOOD AND SEX MAGIC 178
> > *Tantric Sex and the Vampire* *188*
>
> VAMPIRE ETHICS 198

AFTERWORD 210
ABOUT THE AUTHOR 212
APPENDICES 216

Image Credits

Le Vampire by Philip Burne-Jones Bt. (1861-1926)

Lilith by John Collier (1892)

Lord George Gordon Byron, artist unknown

Bram Stoker, photographer unknown

Obsidian Butterfly, Permission for use by Penguin

Vampire Lovers, Hammer Films

Red Vamp, photo provided by model

Anders Manga, permission by Anders Manga

Scarlet, Thearte des Vampires, image provided by Scarlet

Sky, image provided by Vlad, photograph © *Jeffery Grossman*

Chart provided by Suscitatio Enterprises, LLC

Don Henrie, photography by Blood Blood, permission of use granted by Don Henrie

Madame Webb, ©*Madame Webb Photography*

Vampire Wear, photos provided by Joanne of *Vampire Wear*

Vampire Wine, photos used by permission by *Vampire Wine*

Photo provided by *Eva Morgan,* model

Vintage photo, contributed by Merticus of Atlanta Vampire Alliance

Erzbet Bathory, artist unknown

Peter Kurten, photographer unknown

Psychopathia Sexualis, photographer unknown

Courtesy © Fracture 2006 Nightmare Photography, of model Jamie Mahon

Courtesy of model *Sin Whore*, copyright Butler Photography.

Vampires Today, provided by author Joe Laycock and publisher

Vampires in their own words provided by author Michelle Belanger

Onyx, photo courtesy of model.

Psychic Vampire Codex provided by author Michelle Belanger

Acknowledgments

I would like to thank the following people for their undying support and guidance; without their assistance and inspiration this volume would not have been possible.

To Starr for putting in long hours and incredible amounts of patience discussing vampires in all sorts of media and editing. To Michelle Belanger, for the inspiration of the book itself and her commentary while creating it. To my friend and brother Don Henrie for his thoughts and image use. To Jack Sovel, best friend and manager one could ever ask for. Merticus of Suscitatio Enterprises, LLC, the Atlanta Vampire Alliance, and Voices of the Vampire Community, Lenore and Perdition of The Lost Children of the Oubliette, Lono, Lorenzo, Khan, Miss Jenny, Raven Digitalis, Fyre, Adam Jackson, Professor Mike Flohr, for your assistance in Composition I, Professor Kim Autrey for her assistance during and after Public Speaking class, Professor Vic Williamson for commentary and pointers in Sociology, Professor Kevin Eads for your support and engaging discussions, Tim Wright, Britt, Cindi and her daughter Carolyn (Kit) for editing and preproduction commentary, to authors Katherine Ramsland and Martin Riccardo, whose books and commentary helped inspire this work, and to Packrat

Rasor for his enormous generosity, humor and support. And to the vast amount of readers, reviewers and interviewees, all of you have my eternal gratitude.

Foreword

The Dominion of the Vampire
by Merticus

Could the vampire, a creature renowned through the ages for draining the essence of life, hold sway over our carnal proclivities? To understand the vampire you must be willing to explore not only his folkloric influence throughout many of the world's customs, art, literature, and film, but to delve deeper into what the archetype represents against the backdrop of the human psyche. Our personal identity has been rattled, our place as the dominant predator challenged, and our exploration of dark desires and sexual depravity liberated. The true power of the vampire rests not in his proficiency at extinguishing life, but in his ability to transubstantiate our fears into enticing visions of lust, pleasure, and even pain.

As our global society continues to blend, so does the vampire transform across our various artistic mediums. Contemporary portrayals rarely depict the vampire as an undead monster creeping at night from the grave or as an aristocrat methodically choosing his prey through the centuries. The vampire has come to represent an idiosyncratic embodiment of the unabashed strength, beauty, and sexuality that's for too long been repressed within our own culture. We're vicariously living out our fantasies through an adaptation of vampirism cast onto the human condition.

The vampire's eyes pierce the soul and their fangs penetrate the flesh in search of the life they no longer possess. The body, drained of blood and vital energy, goes limp and the breath becomes shallow. As terrifying as this may seem, there's a current of sexual energy and magnetism to their actions. An exchange often occurs that creates a symbiotic bond between the vampire and his prey. While the vampire may exercise suggestion, mesmerism, or mastery of will over their subject, these methods are irrelevant to the outcome. A victim will undoubtedly succumb to their insatiable hunger; the only question is if mutual gratification will be shared equally among them.

We must be willing to ask ourselves what role we play in modifying our conception of the vampire, while not dismissing the possibility that this shifting of the vampire archetype may indeed be self-altering. Some will reject this as a bastardization of the classical vampire and argue that there is nothing glamorous or sensual to be inferred from a bloodsucker. This narrow view on the evolving etymology alienates the progressive yearning for the vampire to increasingly transgress the boundaries placed on them in folklore and myth. Corvis Nocturnum in *Allure of the Vampire*, fortunately doesn't force us to accept one version of the vampire as superior to another.

Corvis explores the early foundations of the vampire mythos; alluding to the presence of the vampire as an influential force in shaping our fears and unspoken desires throughout history. Whether you're intrigued by the barbarous acts of Vlad Tepes, enraptured by the words of Lord Byron, or in shock by the insanity of Elizabeth Bathory and others who've committed atrocities, it's difficult to deny the philosophical underpinnings of the vampire present in their minds. However, vampirism doesn't have to assume a macabre form. Soon you'll travel through a labyrinth of cinematic depictions of the vampire with such memorable films as *The Hunger, Lost Boys,* and *Interview with the Vampire*. Some of the films discussed in *Allure of the Vampire* are lighthearted, using a combination of various comedic devices and absurd sexual perversion to entice the audience.

There's no mistaking that the vampire has permeated almost every facet of our lives from the clothes we wear, the times we spend curled up with a book, to the moments we hold our breath in suspense at the theatre. We're bombarded with images of the vampire through edgy advertisements, couture fashions, and even fine works of art that use blood as a constituent. Musical performers have likewise embraced this nocturnal vision and composed melodic arrangements to arouse our senses. The vampire has even crept into our bedrooms with erotic films, sexual roleplaying games, and adventures into the erotic art of biting. In fact, there is an entire discipline of academic study devoted to deviant leisure, of which vampirism is an emerging category.

Corvis delves deeper than most other authors dare to tread, exposing the real vampire subculture from the perspective of self-identified vampires. His unique position within the vampire community has allowed him access to some of the more influential and artistically gifted among this unique group. Human beings who self-identify as real psychic, sanguinarian (blood-drinking), or living vampires *(vampyres)* reside all around us. Others go further to classify themselves by the types of energy they feed from such as elemental, astral, and sexual. Rather than dismiss them as individuals who've lost touch with reality, consider them an outgrowth from Goth culture, or falsely insinuate that their behavior is harmful or dangerous, they are treated with the utmost deference and fairness.

It's true that many real vampires choose to lurk in silence, remaining underground or hiding in plain sight from their mainstream counterparts. We're not yet at a point in our civilization where we're willing to accept that individuals walk among us who share common elements with the traditional vampire. Perchance, the acceptance or even tolerance of these individuals may be reached in our lifetime; possibly then can the rest of the world catch up to their enlightenment. In the meantime, real vampires will continue to dispel rumors and misconceptions about who they are. They will stress the adherence to responsible ethics as central to the safety of the community and openly voice that the donor should never be ancillary to the vampire.

Real human living vampires are often the most intriguing and multi-faceted persons you're likely to ever come across in your lifetime. Many are endowed with the ability to perceive the emotions of others, visualize constructs to aid in achieving goals, are intuitively aware when something's amiss, raise the energy levels of those around them, and are skilled at bringing their lovers to intense heightened states of sexual pleasure. Some real vampires flirt with a dark aesthetic while surrounding themselves with sophisticated indulgences and an appreciation of intellectual discourse. Should you ever have the opportunity to hold an audience with a vampire such as these, you may come away with a distinctive insight into the world you never possessed before.

The debate over the possible origin of vampirism is by no means settled with some considering it to be an undiagnosed medical condition, genetic alteration, neurobiological, spiritual, or even metaphysical state of being. Despite these various postulations, there exists within these individuals attributes and talents absent from those who are non-vampiric. Drawing from my own involvement with the three-year study of vampirism through the *Vampirism & Energy Work Research Study* conducted by Suscitatio Enterprises, LLC, I've come to the understanding that real vampirism encapsulates elements unique to some that could never be neatly categorized. Corvis addresses this dilemma by presenting a cross-section of ideas and beliefs from the real vampire community in hopes of enveloping the largest possible representation for someone unfamiliar with the subculture.

Corvis is not afraid to broach the subject of sadomasochism or even the magickal properties of blood. The power of the submissive and the trust given to the dominate parallels some the relationships we've seen between vampires and humans in recent storylines such as Stephenie Meyer's *Twilight*. The imagery of blood is sometimes more than just symbolic of life; rather it is the source from which some claim to derive sexual satisfaction. Distinctions between blood-fetishists and sanguinarian (blood-drinking) vampires who profess to imbibe blood to sate a corporeal need, as opposed to a desire, are properly delineated in this work. Many eclectic spiritualists and chaos practitioners use the concept of the vampire as a powerful egregore in their beliefs and practices. Our culture is increasingly embarking into seemingly bizarre and ethereal territory. Those who recognize the underlying role the vampire plays may soon be ushering us along these once hidden paths.

After you've wound your way through the stories, the imagination, the creativity, and the overt sexuality of the vampire in all his forms, you're presented with the means to turn the key and step into the shadows yourself. The resources contained in the appendix allow both novices and adepts alike to pursue more detailed studies into the history of the vampire and real vampirism. In effect, a roadmap to exploring the real vampire subculture is introduced. If you happen to be wandering the streets of New York, Paris, Amsterdam, Prague, or other enchanting cities of the world and come across a real vampire, bestow upon them a measure of benevolence and they may be willing to share with you far more than just a mysterious smile.

The vampire will continue to exist as an allegorical entity, servicing a multiplicity of societal demands and expectations. The fact that we wish to intimately connect with the vampire instead of banishing him illuminates the lascivious mindset of our age and perhaps even a weaknesses inherent to our hearts. Others works may lay claim to a treatise on the psychology of vampire influence, but few of these will leave you questioning what role you've played in elevating the vampire to prominence. *Allure of the Vampire* accomplishes this and so much more; drawing upon a wealth of knowledge and personal experience.

Introduction

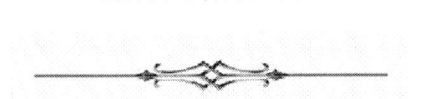

I've always been fascinated by vampires in any form. I recall reading Bram Stoker's classic back in middle school for the first time. Years later I was asked to give my first ever oral book report and I chose Stoker's *Dracula*. The report was conducted totally from memory yet I received an A, so vivid had the memories been. I suppose my subject of choice was telling of the type person I was to become later on in life. My grandmother traveled with gypsies playing Vaudeville and, like her, I had a fascination with the supernatural at an early age, so it made perfect sense to me, now that I look back on my influences. From interest in this tale grew a love of Gothic art and architecture, as well as the supernatural and the occult. I read constantly, devouring book after book and have since added many films to my list of must haves over the years. My own style of artwork was inspired by visits to Hot Topic, scanning the creations of Monolith Graphics featuring the work of Joseph Vargo. I was enthralled by his stone gargoyles and vampires. I collected magazines and calendars by this wonderful artist who drew me into the misty and darkly macabre world, as I did the art books of Brom,

Luis Royo and others. Later, these interests led me to open an occult shop with a darker side to it (now a larger store and magazine, The Ninth Gate) and fueled the desire to write about people who are into various "darker" things. *Embracing the Darkness; Understanding Dark Subcultures* was the result of that effort, complete with a chapter on the vampire subculture.

During this time I became close friends with vampire author Michelle Belanger, and Don Henrie, the popular television icon who walked onto the screen, instantly seeming to embody our conception of the vampire archetype. As discussions with other Elders and members of the online community over the next four years continued and I researched more, I felt my initial work had only scratched the surface. In fact, most of my writings since have been deeper explorations into all the ideas contained within my original work, detailing the key elements in greater length.

Yet, with all the other fictional and folkloric books out there on vampires, *how exactly* would mine be different, I asked myself. I came to realize, that although many books briefly touched on the subject of our sexual attraction and the seductive qualities of these nocturnal creatures, none that even came close have fully done the job as thoroughly as I wanted to do. From folklore, psychology and certainly in erotic fiction and film, sexuality seemed almost blatant, so I began compiling research to explain this fascination we have with the hominus noctum! Vampires have caused our hearts to race at campfire tales, while reading penny dreadfuls in days long before television was even conceived of and became even more embedded upon our collective awareness after silent films like Nosferatu. Artwork graces the covers of books, back in the day and in the here and now, to the extent they even have been the subject of a few different comics and painted graphic novels.

My inspiration for the chapter on deviant behavior was taken from a work in the 1800's, *Psychopathic Sexualis*, which was on sexuality and disturbed minds. The segment on blood fetish rang very close to the other stories I have discovered, from newspaper archives to Katherine Ramsland's encounters back when she first descended into the seductive and terrifying world of New York's search for the reality of vampires in our time. In using a similar name for chapter four, I felt it fitting, as much of our attraction to vampires is both commonly accepted but yet to others a clinical obsession. The mind of those involved in living as vampires was equally intriguing even with the random criminal element, so I included much on the rich and mysterious community that thrives in major cities across every continent and, unfortunately, the shocking incidents that sadly give the vampire world a bad rap.

By using parts of all of these thoughts I started to weave together a very vast amount of material into a single book, which I offer you here as my best effort the most complete volume on the idea to date, spanning our sexual attraction to and for the undead from our earliest fables to the vibrant nightlife of our present times. Thus, it is with great pleasure I offer you the results of my research.

Will our love for vampires ever end? I sincerely doubt it. As long as we ourselves long for immortality and power over what secretly makes us afraid in the dark, we will always yearn for the embrace of the vampire, to share their mastery over the unknown.

                                                                  `Corvis`
                                                                   `Nocturnum`

Allure of the Vampire by Corvis Nocturnum

Le Vampire by Philip Burne-Jones Bt. (1861-1926)

Chapter One

Vampires in Folklore and Early Fiction

Do you hear them? The Children of the Night, what sweet music they make. ~ Dracula

Vampires. Just the mere mention of the vampires puts images into the minds of those who hear the word. Visions of seducers stalking in the dark quicken the heartbeat, in fear and something else equally primal.

In watching or reading about vampires, we vicariously live through them. As voyeurs we're just as excited as the predator. How exactly though, did we as people go from being afraid of the shrouded walking dead with the likes of such as the grotesque Nosferatu to lusting after the modern archetype of vampires like Elvira, Vampirella, Lestat and so many others? Vampires have for centuries drawn us into their embrace, exuding charisma and sexuality, from the piercing gaze of onscreen leading men such as Bela Lugosi, Christopher Lee, Gary Oldman, and so many more. Women and men both have desired to be victims and or lovers to the undead in countless fantasies, lusting after a suave, powerful male or mesmerized by the eyes, lips and cleavage of the vixens in the night. Our culture is inundated with a mental perception on what a vampire should be, how it acts, and despite of (or maybe because of) the fear of peril, we secretly wish we could be one of them. As children we may hide while watching, or as adults hold our dates mesmerized by the actors who hold us in their thrall as surely as they do their onscreen victims.

A young woman I spoke to described vampires and sexuality by saying the following:

Vampires are a seduction of the mind, body, and soul. They sexualize death in an aspect unlike any other. Their suave manor and dark ways, lure us to the heart of our very darkest desires. The ultimate sacrifice of lust and love for them, is not life, but in truth a death. An encounter in the dark, the caress of a lovers breath on the neck or wrist, the need to embrace that which we fear, a midnight rendezvous, the cool touch as their fingers glide across your eager flesh, and the knowledge that you are truly being seduced by death himself. Such a creature, surrounded in a shroud of night and mystery, dancing the razors edge of all that we are, couldn't be anything but Sexual.

From a Vampire's point of view, we are the very nature of sexual desire. We use lust as a tool, to cultivate that which we want in others. We caress and tease and make you beg for all that we are offering. We offer the seduction of ages past, of things undiscovered within, the slightest taste of fear to chase your dreams into the night. Our eternal kiss allows you to embrace death and seek the darkest corners of your soul. We are your darkest desires. ~Jessica Rose 'Fyre Dancer'

Early superstitions

Nearly every culture in the world has had its own particular version of a vampire, even if the name or various features are different. In the following sections, we'll explore the majority of the ones that shaped our modern image of them and how sexuality eventually came to play a part in reshaping our views from monstrosity to a figure of desire.

Lilith, mother of all Succubi

In *The Book of Lilith* the author goes into great detail on her Jewish origins. Jewish people were slaves in Egypt and while there they assimilated the ideas of the ancient Babylonians. From the *Book of Isaiah* and in the *Talmud* she was known as the Lamia, or witch. She was later given the aspects of the screech owl around the time of King James Version of the Bible. Identified as the progenitor of all Incubi and Succubi, which were male and female demons who would prey on slumbering people for sex most stories of Lilith depict her as the first wife of Adam.

Late medieval Jewish legend she subsequently became the mother of demons, called Lilin. A Hebrew tradition that exists still in which an amulet inscribed with the names of three angels was placed around the neck of newborn boys in order to protect them until circumcision. It was also Hebrew tradition to wait three years before a boy's hair was cut so as to attempt to trick Lilith into thinking the child is a girl so that the males would be safe. Lilith was thought to be the mother of Cain, as well as the goddess Hecate because she is the dark power of feminine witchcraft. A good many writers identify old folklore with Lilith, such as Crowley and Gerald Gardner. Gardner, the 1950's Wicca founder, who asserted that there was continuous historical worship of Lilith to our present day, and that her name is sometimes given to the goddess being personified in the coven, by the priestess. Lilith is viewed as the embodiment of the goddess like Isis, Ishtar and Hecate.

A vampire community elder named Khan, whom I met via the Voices of the Vampire Community meeting, expressed one of the best comments on the incubus:

My own personal thought is that this creature was invented to explain men and women waking from erotic dreams. It was simple to explain an erection or wet spot to your spouse in the morning by claiming you were demonically possessed by an incubus or succubus (the female version). Such a horrible beast would be easy to detract from the shame of dreaming about sex during such a time when it was considered sinful enough for punishment.

According to a conversation with an online friend, "In modern times, it is usually thought of as one who feeds from sexual energy, the way a psychic vampire feeds from chi, or a sanguine vampire feeds from blood. The general perception is that the incubus or succubus feeds off either the energy created from sexual tension, or the energy created by sexual activity." Lilith personifies this trait for the feminine vampire, in fiction and among the living vampires of our modern day subculture.

Other cultures

As far back as Sumerian culture vampire styled creatures existed, about five thousand years ago, the

Mesopotamians had stories of *Lamastu*, a winged creature whose name meant "she who erases." Lamastu liked to suck the blood of young men, leaving them diseased, sterile and prone to nightmares. The ancient Chinese vampires, called *Chiang-shih*, and because of them the dead were buried with their toes tied so that they would be slowed down in the pursuit of the living. Germany had *Blutsaugers*, who were reanimated corpses, (usually suicide victims,) although reportedly you could also become a Blutsauger if a nun jumped over your grave. In Malaysian folklore, the *Pontianak* was a female vampire whose head could separate from her body, with its entrails dangling from the base of her neck. Within Philippine folklore, the *Manananggal* was a female vampire whose entire upper body could separate from her lower body who could fly using wings, and sucked the blood of fetuses. They also told of the *Aswang*. The Aswang is believed to always be a female of considerable beauty by day and, by night, a fearsome flying fiend. The Aswang lives in a house, can marry and have children, a seemingly normal human during the daylight hours. Bulgaria had a vampire which had only one nostril, slept with its left eye open and its thumbs linked. It was also held responsible for cattle plagues. In Moravia, vampires were fond of throwing off their shrouds and attacking their victims in the nude. Most modern Western notions of vampirism derive primarily from Eastern

European lore. The *Striga* of ancient Rome carried its presence forward into the rest of the known European world, and the Romanians believed Nosferat, later changed to Nosferatu, came to the slumbering people as attractive visitors in the night. As did the legends of the *Succubi*, the *Nosferat* had sex with the slumbering villagers. The Slavic folk stories told of the creature called *Mora*, a vampire who becomes obsessed with their victims after having ingested their blood. Old gypsy tales presented a very sexual vampire, perhaps this was the source for those in Bram Stoker's Dracula (and subsequent copies of the story) of the female companions of Dracula that seduced Jonathan Harker.

Katherine Ramsland, a professor of forensic psychology at DeSales University in Pennsylvania and author of *The Science of Vampires*, cited the works of J. Gordon Melton, who indicates this sexually aroused vampire, at least in the males, might have been due to the discovery of male corpses with erections. It simply carried over to the females as having been similarly capable to perform. Europe may have the largest collection of creatures of the night; in nearly all other societies have their share of vampires. In modern times it has been speculated that the fallen angels mentioned in the Book of Enoch, the Nephilim, bore resemblance to vampires in power and deeds, but the debate continues.

The Dark Romantics

Things drastically changed as far as vampires go during the time of the Romantic Period. Far from being loathsome creatures lurking in shadows decaying by day and shambling into homes by night terrorizing rustic medieval Europe, blood drinkers suddenly saw a shift towards the mesmerizing to the seductive, androgynous creature of power and beauty, the sex symbols we think of today. *"Vampires are connected with sexuality in a way that other monsters like Frankenstein, zombies and werewolves are not,"* said Amy Kind, an associate professor of philosophy at Claremont McKenna College in Claremont, east of Los Angeles. *"The bite of the vampire, the transfer of blood, is intimate, and the sexual overtones are often not very far from the surface."*

In 1797 Goethe penned the poem *The Bride of Cornith*, a vampiric short tale which influenced John Keats to write *Lamia*, based off Lilith as the mother of succubi. Prominent in the history of vampire literature for the fact it heralded sexuality in the form of a lesbian tale of in 1801 was Samuel Taylor Coleridge's poem *Christabel*. His description of the female vampire is this:

There she sees a damsel bright,
Dressed in a silken robe of white,
That shadowy in the moonlight shone :

The neck that made that white robe wan,
Her stately neck, and arms were bare ;
Her blue-veined feet unsandal'd were ;
And wildly glittered here and there
The gems entangled in her hair.
I guess, 'twas frightful there to see
A lady so richly clad as she--
Beautiful exceedingly!

And later on in the poem Coleridge continues as the woman is seduced to disrobe for the vampiress:

Do love you, holy Christabel !
And you love them, and for their sake
And for the good which me befel,
Even I in my degree will try,
Fair maiden, to requite you well.
But now unrobe yourself ; for I
Must pray, ere yet in bed I lie.

Quoth Christabel, So let it be !
And as the lady bade, did she.
Her gentle limbs did she undress
And lay down in her loveliness.

But through her brain of weal and woe

So many thoughts moved to and fro,
That vain it were her lids to close ;
So half-way from the bed she rose,
And on her elbow did recline
To look at the lady Geraldine.

Beneath the lamp the lady bowed,
And slowly rolled her eyes around ;
Then drawing in her breath aloud,
Like one that shuddered, she unbound
The cincture from beneath her breast :
Her silken robe, and inner vest,
Dropt to her feet, and full in view,
Behold ! her bosom, and half her side-- --
A sight to dream of, not to tell !
O shield her ! shield sweet Christabel !

The year 1818 saw the publication of *La Belle Dame sans Merci* by Keats. Charles Baudelaire, whom I wrote much on it *Promethean Flame*, wrote *Les Metamorphoses du Vampire* in 1857. *Jungle Book* author Rudyard Kipling did *The Vampire* first exhibited at the new gallery in London in 1897.

A fool there was and he made his prayer
(Even as you and I!)
To a rag and a bone and a hank of hair

(We called her the woman who did not care),
But the fool he called her his lady fair
(Even as you and I!)
Oh the years we waste and the tears we waste
And the work of our head and hand,
Belong to the woman who did not know
(And now we know that she never could know)
And did not understand.
A fool there was and his goods he spent
(Even as you and I!)
Honor and faith and a sure intent
But a fool must follow his natural bent
(And it wasn't the least what the lady meant),
(Even as you and I!)
Oh the toil we lost and the spoil we lost
And the excellent things we planned,
Belong to the woman who didn't know why
(And now we know she never knew why)
And did not understand.
The fool we stripped to his foolish hide
(Even as you and I!)
Which she might have seen when she threw him aside--
(But it isn't on record the lady tried)
So some of him lived but the most of him died--
(Even as you and I!)

And it isn't the shame and it isn't the blame
That stings like a white hot brand.
It's coming to know that she never knew why
(Seeing at last she could never know why)
And never could understand.

Lord Byron

George Gordon Noel Byron was born on January 22, 1788. He was a poet and leading figure in Romanticism. Byron's mark in history was not only due to his writings, but also on his life, which featured extravagant living, and vast amount of affairs, enormous debts and allegations of incest and sodomy. A study in contrasts, this melancholy satirist and aristocratic champion of the common person, handsome and adored but obsessed with a small personal deformity. Byron fled England to escape scandal and a failed marriage and died of fever in 1824. His natural gift for poetry was the only consistency in his troubled life. Yet even during his lifetime, his personal life overshadowed his work. However, in my opinion Byron equaled Stoker as a crucial influence on the vampire mythos in our times. His epic poem *The Giaour* written in 1813, is an early example of vampire influence.

> *But thou, false Infidel! shalt writhe*
> *Beneath avenging Monkir's scythe;*
> *And from its torment 'scape alone*
> *To wander round lost Eblis' throne;*
> *And fire unquenched, unquenchable,*
> *Around, within, thy heart shall dwell;*
> *Nor ear can hear nor tongue can tell*
> *The tortures of that inward hell!*
> *But first, on earth as vampire sent,*
> *Thy corse shall from its tomb be rent:*
> *Then ghastly haunt thy native place,*
> *And suck the blood of all thy race;*
> *There from thy daughter, sister, wife,*
> *At midnight drain the stream of life;*
> *Yet loathe the banquet which perforce*
> *Must feed thy livid living corse:*
> *Thy victims ere they yet expire*
> *Shall know the demon for their sire,*
> *As cursing thee, thou cursing them,*
> *Thy flowers are withered on the stem.*

Fellow Dark Moon Press author Michelle Belanger told me of Byron: *Everyone learns about him in high school English* class, and his ideas and philosophies had a huge impact upon the Romantic Movement, but there are so many aspects of his life that are typically censored. He had an open fascination with magick and the occult. Reportedly, he ran Black Masses out of his family's estate, Newstead Abbey, a manor that is still reputed to be haunted. He dug up the skull of a monk from that self-same abbey and had it turned into a grisly chalice. He got his hands on the mysterious Book of Enoch, a forbidden lost book of the Bible banned by the Church of his day, only a few years after that book had even made it into the English language. Throughout the course of his life, he identified as a vampire, a pirate, a fallen angel, and even the Devil himself. It's no wonder Byron, all by his lonesome, is pretty much the proto-type of the modern Gothic movement. That and he was openly bisexual in a time when sex between two men was still punishable by death in England. You just won't find a much more Luciferian figure who lived by his ideals right up until his tragic, early death at age thirty-six.

Palidori

In 1819 Byron's physician, Polidori, in a work of fiction, based one of the earliest incarnations of the ruthless yet romantic vampire off of Lord Byron. The Italian doctor, who attempted many times to become more than friends with the other man, was spurned and went back and forth expressing in his writings from love to hate. This was no doubt part of the early ambiguous sexual leanings that vampires have always exuded, in both males and females alike, from then till now. The movies *The Haunted Summer* and *Gothic* depicting Byron, Palidori and Mary Shelley gave us a look at life during that time and their personalities.

One of the first fictional vampires influenced by the character Lord Ruthven was *Varney the Vampire* penned by James Malcolm Rymer who also wrote *Sweeny Todd* during the 1840's in penny dreadfulls, which were weekly magazines. In it Sir Francis Varney prowled Europe as the vampire aristocrat stalking lushious women. Alexandre Dumas author of *The Three Musketeers*, *The Man in the Iron Mask* and *The Count of Monte Cristo* (a favorite film of mine) wrote a vampire story laced with erotic overtones in 1848 called *The Pale Lady*. It is difficult to find, but well worth reading.

Carmilla

In 1872 novel *Carmilla* by Le Fanu is about a nineteenth century story recanting the life of Carmilla, a succubus who enters nineteen year old Laura's bedroom, after becoming close to the family and gradually seducing the daughter by holding hands and kissing over time. Taking the younger girl's blood while she sleeps and inflicting nightmares while doing so, she continued her conquest gradually. *Carmilla* influenced the female vampire for generations, yet this work is known by scholars far more than by the common vampire reader. Still, our views on the female vampire remains shrouded in mystery compared to the typical cookie cutter male vampire of Dracula, Lestat, etc. She is perceived to be the symbol of female liberation in a period of complete patriarchy yet she has both sexuality and a cunning nature that was seen as the direct opposite of the status quo of Victorian women. In behaving as she did, the vampiress behaviour caused a sense of fear in men due to the power she possessed. This dark femme fatale could seduce men and women alike, and while the male vampire is a frightening figure to men because he can show women their masculinity, the female vampire, on the other hand, is capable of rendering her victims, especially the male character helpless. We all know that the misogynistic, all powerful male *must* prevail and never show weakness, thus, masculinity of the female goes against Victorian standards; and has to be destroyed. James B. Twitchell says in his work, *The Living Dead: A Study of the Vampire in Romantic Literature,* that *...the femme fatale is wonderfully attractive...but she is too powerful, too threatening to the male ego. Hence, she can only be an 'object' of male fantasy, not reality.*

"We can look at vampires in literature and cinema as an empty vessel that can be filled up with any of a variety of contemporary issues," said Peter Logan, a professor of English at Temple University in Philadelphia and an authority on Victorian literature. "They're a tool with multiple uses, and clearly one that continues to be meaningful in different ways to a new generation."

As in all things, change is inevitable and yet, the main facets of the primal hunter always remain intact. In every era the vampire sought his or her prey no matter the look or time period they have been set in.

Bram Stoker

I would certainly be remiss if I didn't include Stoker and his creation when writing of sexuality. In his own lifetime, Stoker was better known as the personal assistant of actor Henry Irving and business manager of the Lyceum Theatre in London, which Irving owned. But in 1897, the author drew on Romanian vampire folklore in creating the classic novel *Dracula,* and with it Bram Stoker detailed one of the most memorable night stalkers ever created. From the earliest of copies in print to films using the name Dracula, the world more than likely would not have become so enamored with vampires without him. Bram Stoker's work ironically gave way to countless films that used the name Dracula, even if they diverted from the original story.

In order to see the full extent of the impact that has rippled across time from the creation of the infamous character, Dracula, we need to study the influences of the period and personal influences of the writer himself. *Dracula* was written during epidemic disease, contagion, bizarre and unknown mental illnesses, and the public emergence of sexuality, especially among women. One female fan explained about Stoker's attitude on women in his writing thus,

If you go back to Stoker's book, as I am sure that you are aware, it is the red headed woman (one of the three sisters in the castle) who stands up to Dracula. It is actually Mina not Van Helsing who causes his downfall l- and not totally intentionally - she is fulfilling social obligation to her husband (loyalty) by protecting Jonathan, who is boring and weak as a character from page one) from her more sensual side that Dracula invokes in her. If you recall, she cries "Unclean, unclean..." when she is burned by the symbol of conventional morality in the form of the Host of the Christian communion. I feel that Mina is never going to be truly happy again even after the conclusion of the book because she has seen what is out there. She will do her duty and lay back and think of England but it does not evoke that same spark that she found with Dracula. That, at least in her fantasies, she becomes less Nora from A

Dolls House and more Anna Karenina without the tragic ending as she will safely remain in her box in this life. It is what is expected.

Victorian times

The old stereotype of the Victorians as afraid of sex, especially the denial and repression of women's sexuality, is largely distorted. The truth is that they were probably even more obsessed with sex than we modern vampire fans are, but, unlike people today, considered it inappropriate to talk about it.

When he was a congressman, Theodore Roosevelt was close friends with both Stoker and playwright and author Oscar Wilde. Both men visited Roosevelt's estate on Long Island, and Stoker continued to visit Roosevelt in the White House. Reading the description of Dracula's protagonist, Teddy Roosevelt bore a striking resemblance to the character, Van Helsing. Both were Dutch scientists, and I found on one book on Stokers past, the Roosevelt's hated vampires. Teddy Roosevelt was quite vocal in his protest against what he called "degenerate effects of female sexuality," and was upset at aspects of Rudyard Kipling's poem *The Vampire*, writing once that "it always struck me as being in a decadent tone."

Some historical vampirologists say that Teddy Roosevelt influenced the character Van Helsing, at least in part. The person that stood in the way of Dracula was Van

Helsing, the vampire hunter upon whom others would be based, slaying all that was evil, as surely as did knights against dragons, or Don Quixote pitting himself against windmills. Stoker's friend, President Theodore Roosevelt, clashed with the immorality of his day. Long Islander Walt Whitman represented everything that was evil and indecent because he was a proponent of the ungodly. Walt Whitman started what turned into a worldwide sexually decadent movement. Originally, Stoker was enamored by Walt Whitman and his sexually charged poems. The fictional character Dracula took on not only the likeness of Whitman's physical attributes, but represented his sexually seductive nature. *Dracula*, it is speculated, is a mirror of what Stoker saw in the world as "a seduction of society by evil writers." Towards the end of his life Stoker publicly condemned writers that included sex in their books. I find that quite a hypocritical turnaround from when he was younger and quite publicly promoted the writings of Whitman. Bram Stoker's grand-nephew said "that he (Stoker) died of syphilis that he got from loose sex." Perhaps the knowledge that he was dying from this sexually transmitted disease, which was common to both genders, was the reason for his change of heart. Suspiciously his relationship with his wife was sexless, yet Bram Stoker's wife was the former lover of Oscar Wilde, who was famously persecuted for his bisexuality!

In one biography, it allegedly details the unrequited desires of not only Stoker to Whitman, but also to Washington Irving – the very same man Stoker had in mind to play the character of Dracula on stage. Irving's piercing gaze and charismatic manner certainly were attributes vampires repeatedly seem to possess. So, to clarify a bit Bram Stoker took Whitman's look and sexuality, combined with Irving's demeanor to create Dracula and, simultaneously, Van Helsing was his own frustration, coupled with Roosevelt's purity! I allege the Stoker was slaying his own unrequited feelings for people in having Van Helsing kill Dracula.

I suggest reading Barbra Belford's book published in 1996 entitled *Bram Stoker a Biography and the man who was Dracula*. To some theorists the book Dracula is a warning to people not to follow Whitman's example. Certainly there are various flavors of barely repressed homoeroticism lurking beneath the surface of Stoker's novel. Lord Byron may have been the earliest homosexual and bisexual influence on vampires, Anne Rice was the most obvious one, but perhaps the biggest influence was the closeted homophobic Stoker. Dracula's creator allegedly wrote love letters to Walt Whitman, the hero and friend of his younger days. Stoker may have been making a parallel point in showing that Whitman's poetry was victimizing society with his erotic ways in much the same manner as Dracula to his victims. As with his early feelings for both Whitman and Irving, I see other parallels myself. I also thought it a good idea to note the similarities between Lord Byron and Palidori in the love/ hate and Stoker and *his* interests. Lord Byron may have been a pansexual dandy that influenced modern vampires, which is amusing because that could describe that famous roommate Stoker had who fits that description as well – Oscar Wilde. I speculate those conflicts contributed to his drinking and morality-laden tale condemning the loose desires of women. Or men, if my conclusions are correct.

Stoker seems to be a bit confusing in his own views on a good many points in his classic, for in many places in *Dracula*, he contradicts popular views of gender and at other times reinforces them. In the appendix of the Penguins Classics version there are many details that describe the viewpoint that is portrayed in *Dracula* from respected Victorian authors, historians, and scientists, as well as Stoker himself. They claim that this rigid role of stereotypes was vital to the success of gender relations and even to society as a whole; those who lived outside these edicts were seen as degenerates, as was (and still is) a part of alternative sexuality today. Gender blurring is shown by Mina and Lucy, but also by the men in the novel. As with Jonathan Harker and female vampires in Dracula's castle, the sexual roles are reversed, and given the misogynistic attitude of the times, a woman who takes control of her sexuality is considered evil. Jonathan is victim to three vampire women while at Dracula's abode. As he waits with eyes closed in "languorous ecstasy…with beating heart" for one of the vixens to bite him, the Count arrives and in a rage exclaims: "How dare you touch him, any of you? How dare you cast eyes on him when I have forbidden it? Back, I tell you all! This man belongs to me! Beware how you meddle with him, or you'll have to deal with me…Yes. I too can love…I promise you that when I am done with him you shall kiss him at your will."

There are also other situations in which the men in the story taking on feminine qualities. This feminine feature is seen in Van Helsing after Lucy's death while in the carriage with Dr. Seward. Van Helsing went into hysterics, crying "just as a woman does," Stoker chauvinistically describes. Here, in his depiction, Stoker is once again giving his male protagonist feminine characteristics.

The male/female gender role reversals, the seeming contradictions in Stoker's own work makes it seem that he was unsure of his exact views on the subject. It can also be seen as a reflection of the views of the day and age he lived in. The fact that *Dracula* was such a success could lend itself to the fact that people were intrigued by their sexuality, although it was "wrong." Stoker is in line with Victorian beliefs when his novel is taken at face value. But Stoker also seems to share the underlying curiosity of the age, giving alternative views on sexuality their just due, while maintaining the accepted view on the surface. Quite often his vampires blur the concept of gender, stimulating a fear of vampire sexuality, a phenomenon in which gender roles evolved in a complicated manner. Men become feminine as victims are penetrated by the vampire's phallic fangs; women take on the stereotypical masculine trait of aggressive sexuality. Bisexuality contributes to the terrifying threat Stoker and his nineteenth-century readers saw in vampirism. Even members of the real vampire subculture tend to represent diverse sexual identities not only with many who view gender as fluid, but also with some refusing to recognize themselves as either male or female. Disproportionate to the general population, a number of individuals in this subculture are actually transgendered. Still many others are practicing pansexualists, or those who share an aesthetic attraction, love, or sexual desire for someone, regardless of their identified gender or biological sex.

Alternative sexuality resurfaces

Various time periods in literature had both lesbian and gay vampires, in works such as the 1800's works Cristabel and Carmilla. In 1966 a film by Roman Polanski called Fearless Vampire Hunters had gay vampires. The 1980's shifted the focus again from heterosexual vampires to a more obvious bisexual and homosexual one. Anne Rice was perhaps the most famous for it, yet she said vampires are outside our morals and boundaries in society. Being outlaws of mortal man's laws and mores by preying on humanity, they break the laws of morality by being sexual and guilt-free with whomever they so chose. Louis and Lestat seem to be a same sex family, when Claudia is brought over and they all live together for years. Armand seems to be extremely drawn to Louis in the first book and film adaptation. A large amount of gay erotica vampire stories came out later, and those in the Goth scene who are gay often enjoy the vampire lifestyle. Rice used to write very explicit erotica, slanted for the BDSM crowd under the pen name A.N. Roquelaure, when she wrote the Sleeping Beauty series, so she has always had a strong interest in the taboo, of various sorts. Perhaps this is also an influence of hers, with the androgynous nature and dress is the aspects that draw bisexual reader in, as she portrays open gender blurring in her characters styles and mannerisms.

    Polyamory, that is to say, the love of many, is evident in Stokers tale. Mina says, "Why can't …a girl marry three men, or as many as want her, and save all this trouble?" Yet, despite the influence of the vampire seducing her and prodding her to think outside of acceptable parameters, she quickly adds, "But this is heresy, and I must not say it."

Dracula himself has three wives, in the original and in the newer version, *Van Helsing,* starring Hugh Jackman. Poppy Z. Brite's story *Soul* contains three-way sex "naked and embracing...drinking blood together, bonding." Author Nancy Kilpartick thinks, "Sex and horror are intertwined, because they are two taboos in society." I agree. Both are satisfying to the audience in the fiction and the voyeuristic viewer. I am not surprised to find that vampire fans tend to be open about their own sexuality, no matter what their chosen lifestyle, sexually speaking. Horror films, vampire lovers, and the like are simply an extension of who and what they are, for the readers share a similar mindset with their favorite characters. Feeling like an outcast is an expected result, cause or after affect in the vampire, Goth, and other similar subcultures, both before and after they become involved in their chosen lifestyles. Many of the stories mentioned here contain elements of bondage and sadomasochism. Once again, the similarities and overlap of all dark cultures is obvious. Many adult vampire films contain similar themes, and many participants in the living vampire lifestyle are also heavily into BDSM, in parts of the bigger cities like New York, Chicago, Las Vegas, and Los Angeles but I'll go into that much later in the last few chapters of this book.

Laurel K. Hamilton

Of all the vampire works of mainstream fiction pushing the envelope on sexuality, Hamilton's does it the most. Her best-selling series, *Anita Blake: Vampire Hunter* is about a female paranormal investigator and her polyandrous relationships with several vampires and an assorted cast of were-creatures. The series spans over a dozen plus novels as well as a number of short story collections and other tie-in media such as graphic novels – large sized comic books. More than 6 million copies of Anita Blake novels have been printed; many of the titles in the series made it to the *New York Times* bestseller list multiple times. Some fans on the online community called Livejournal told me: *"The erotic appeal is a definite attraction. Hamilton's have to have stood out to me the most. They are the first vampire books I really got into. They are the ones that got me hooked. I think some of it is the magic and the mystery, but I've always been a fantasy fan so that's a must for most books. Also there is how much each author's interpretation of vampires differs; it*

keeps every read interesting and unique. Plus they are easier to write in a more realistic setting. The fact that this outrageous fantasy is often written in a realistic world makes it easier to imagine, and (to "a certain extent) believe. Adds to the appeal.

Another LiveJournal user I spoke to agreed totally and added it had a characteristic lacking in other stories; *"Personally, I'm more attracted to the books because of Anita Blake. I wish I was that bad-ass. I'm a bit bad-ass IRL,* (in real life) *but Anita is awesome. We need more novels with strong women as main characters."*

Sometimes readers want to be drawn in because they get to share in the drama, suspending reality, even for a moment in which they too could find romance.

Not everyone is so kind in describing the series however. For some time, many readers have expressed a lack of enthusiasm with Hamilton's increasing focus on her lead character's difficulty with the *ardeur,* that is to say a supernatural hunger necessitating the person to feed it from sexual energy and added metaphysical powers. The *ardeur* seems overly used rather quickly, and the writer uses it to force Anita Blake and her partners into increasingly gratuitous sexual encounters to solve all problems through sex. In the March 26, 2006 review in the *Boston Globe* of *Micah* was largely negative: "..we were not impressed. Hamilton no doubt appeals to romance and erotica lovers, but it does not take long for the clichés and the constant droning about sex to become tiresome." The last few books after *Harlequin* seem to be going back to the original flavor of true character development. Author Michelle Belanger commented on the archetype of the modern vampire is almost oozing with sexuality in keeping with writers like Anne Rice and Laurel K. Hamilton by saying, *"Vampires and sex do seem to go hand in hand, especially these days. There's been this huge glut of vampire-themed romance novels on the market, and this was definitely spear-headed by Hamilton and Rice before her. In Stoker's time, when he was writing Dracula, the vampire in part stood for forbidden sexuality. That forbidden sexuality was part of the vampire's inherent evil, at least as far as nineteenth century authors were concerned. These days, people seem especially fascinated with forbidden sexuality, with pushing the boundaries between pain and pleasure, achieving the experience of something truly extreme. So of course vampires have become a part of that, a potent metaphor for sex and power and immortal beauty and all those things so many people want in their ultimate lover."*

On March 31, 2009 *IFC tv* announced its first original event, *Laurell K. Hamilton's Anita Blake: Vampire Hunter*, the movie begins production this summer which will be produced by *Lionsgate* and *After Dark Films*. Hamilton's work is adapted by Glen Morgan of *X-Files* and *Final Destination* who serves as executive producer.

"I'm thrilled to be bringing my characters and world to television for the first time," stated Hamilton. "*After Dark Films, Lionsgate* and *IFC* all push the boundaries on film. I push the boundaries on paper. I can't wait to see what we can create together." Her next Anita Blake: Vampire Hunter novel, *Skin Trade*, will find its way to stores in June of 2009.

Executive producers are Courtney Solomon of *An American Haunting* and *After Dark's Horrorfest* and Glen Morgan. Laurell K. Hamilton, Jonathan D. Green and Stephanie Caleb are the co-executive producers, and executive vice president and general manager and Evan Shapiro, president of *IFC tv* and *Sundance channel*.

Twilight

It's the story of a human girl, Bella, who falls in love with a 108-year-old vampire who looks seventeen, Edward. Edward is the vampire of our youngest generation, a heartthrob of a school student, and a "vegetarian vampire," that is to say, he resists his inner desire to drink human blood and feasts only on animals instead, a called vegetarian vamp is not new... from Louis devouring rats, to Nick in Forever Knight to Mick St John on last year's US TV series Moonlight, didn't attack poor animals used a blood bank...

Young women are ecstatic over the *Twilight* books, even though they are a total reworking of the highly sexualized vampire tradition. Women of all ages are infatuated with Edward, and even the actor portraying Edward in the films is being mobbed by flocks of women as surly as did Christopher Lee and other Dracula actors. Edward is her protector, and that appeals to a lot of young women. Edward combines the feel of safety, he also has the dangerous aspect, and yet, when Bella does start pushing to have sex with Edward, he decides 'for her own good' that they should wait until they get married. Twilight Moms, as they call themselves, are a very active part of the *Twilight* community, and it seems suggestive that this character, this story, has an appeal. And I think the appeal is the anti-sexuality of the books. It's almost a rejection of sexual promiscuity, with a sense of 'coming of age innocence' feel.

America as a society, if not every controlling society in every generation, attempts to protect its youth from the realities of the world. According to this underlying story, seems to take Stokers preaching of chastity and purity, the saving oneself for marriage is not just "the right thing to do," it's a choice which grants the willing victims a eternal life and everything else the traditional vampire could. It makes me think of the young woman Jessie in *Queen of the Damned* who pursues Lestat, who feels an unbreakable bond. The charisma he holds over her is undeniable, as he is charming and mesmerizing. Lestat seems to have a similar view of the innocence of Jessie when he compares her to the fragile butterfly and why humans in their frailty appeal to him.

Beyond that, other fans explain it has simplistic reasons, along with Rice's works, saying *"...the Twilight Series, vampires are fascinating. Love triangles are always good material. Throw in a werewolf as one side of the triangle, and you've got something that I really don't think has been done before. The author is incredibly talented; I've read her one book outside of the Twilight series and was just as engrossed and entertained. The characters are very real and very relatable; you wish you knew them in real life. Plus, more than Anne Rice, it's cross-generational. The maidens are where this story is happening; the mothers and crones get a fond trip back to their first loves. The only other thing I can think to tell you is that vampire fiction is just plain FUN!! I would love to go to the Lunatic Cafe. Or interview Louie. Or flirt with Lestat. Or Jean Claude (Laurel K. Hamilton's character). Really, if it weren't fun, people wouldn't keep buying it, and with supply and demand working the way it does, it wouldn't be out there."* A valid point, I must agree, as thousands of young women flocked to the theatres during its premiere night. After it sold out within hours, I learned one father had said he didn't even know it was a book until his daughter begged to see it.

Edward suppresses both lusts for blood and his physical desire for Bella, even refusing to kiss her. In this story Bella wanting to join vampires the typical chase is reversed, with a human pursues vampire, and the vampire flees. The excessively glossed over, romanticized vampire meets its peak in yet another way, appealing specifically to women, from women. Contemporary fiction increasingly views the vampire's androgyny and sexual orientation as alluring, even though male vampires these stories usually are incapable of sexual intercourse. Analyzing the impotent male vampire in recent novels of sympathetic vampires, is much like those of Rice's works, suffering from erectile dysfunction yet possessing the immense power to drive women wild. As a fan named Andrea responded to my questionnaire said, *"Vampires attract me because of their strength. Their beauty is seductive. Their power over humans is magically incredible!"* Another fan, Sue, says of the books,

"I originally found vampires to be the most beautiful people in the world. I was a little taken aback at their beauty, grace, intelligence, and ability to love. I was first enchanted by vampires when I read the twilight saga. I was just amazed at Edward's ability to love Bella and stay with her even though her blood was so tempting to him. Then, as their relationship grew, so did my love and respect for vampires. I learned to know what kind of creatures vampires are and the hardships they face. I soon became obsessed and I wanted to find vampires, and have them make me immortal. To this day I still am obsessed with vampires and I still want one to come to me and ask me if I still want it. I would gladly say yes because I would know how to survive and to exist with humans

and I would know the pain it would bring to be near humans but I first would ask them to wait until I turned 18 so I could prove as an adult. But still being a vampire would be the greatest experience for me and I know that vampires are the core of my existence, and that I will always love them. I find vampires to be quite erotic because they can love like no human can, and they know how to make you shiver on a blistering hot day. So in truth, vampires to me are the most amazing creatures, and even though I'll never be able to prove that they truly do exist, I'll always still believe because even if they don't truly exist till I'm 55, lying in a hospital bed, and dying of cancer, I'd still ask for immortality and then I can say to the world but mostly to myself 'see I told u vampires existed!! I knew they did....I knew it' and then if I died I'd die peacefully because then I would know that I finally proved that they existed and I would be happy, for then I would have my one true peace. To have my dying wish come true: me never giving up, and proving that vampires do exist. And then I would continue blissfully into this strange world that I never knew existed."

Sexually speaking, women respond faster than men, usually because they respond from a combination of emotion and the sensory, where otherwise most males are visual and go by their more primal urges. But great lovers in time have all known the secret to a majority of woman is through her feelings and sensations such as touch, how a man smells and looks. Just take a look at your average romance novel cover and it is obvious how the publishers marketing appeals to the fantasized perfect male sweeping the readers off their feet. Romanticized vampires mirror this quality to a large degree.

Saint-Germain is Dracula styled vampire with a difference, a Transylvanian nobleman with most of the traditional vampiric traits, whose feeding brings supreme bliss rather than horror. Vampires provide erotic pleasure, and the sharing through oral gratification, and this manner of depicting vampirism draws on Freudian theory. Saint-Germain also appeals to readers, as well as to female characters within the tales, because his thirst is tied to a craving for intimacy. "It isn't the power and the blood. . . . It is the touching". The author, Chelsea Quinn Yarbro, has a version of vampires are not capable of erection and ejaculation, and cannot become satiated in their feeding unless the human donor reaches orgasm. Saint-Germain makes this clear while explaining to a new vampire that cynically remarks that he expects to get a "good lay" from his first donor. "It is essential that *she* have the good lay. Otherwise you will have nothing." It would seem the joining between vampire and human lovers, both before and after the act, transcends anything between normal humans according to this writer. Different authors use different ways to maintain the vampire's allure, and fictional vampires fall into two types - those that pursue human sexual partners, and those who seek only their own kind.

Romance novels

Women have taken over and a new genre of fiction featuring unearthly gorgeous, 'non-typical male' sensuous, and romantic creatures of the night -- has emerged, using the vampire as the protagonist, bad boy antihero in their romance novels. To be fair, I would class *Twilight* and all of Meyers works as a youth version of this, bridging the gap between the action-fantasy of Hamilton's writings. Amanda, a young woman responding to a questionnaire I put out online spoke of vampires being the ultimate mate, said *"What I find erotic about vampires is the fact that when they love, they do it fiercely and hungrily. It doesn't matter what their love's status in society is, or how much they do or do not have, they devote all their attention to them. They take time to find out what attracts that person and they do all in their power to have them, no matter how many rejections are thrown their way. Jean-Claude's wooing of Anita Blake in Laurell K Hamilton's series is a prime example of this.*

It doesn't matter what they look like; they are suave, debonair, and know just the right thing to say at just the right moment. What wouldn't any woman give to be the center of a man's attention in that way?"

. Certainly the writer of Count Saint-Germain is on the money with his particular version of a vampire, which is detailed in this work. One out of the many books chocking bookstores and Wal-Mart (I noted many while shopping late one night) was by psychotherapist Lynda Hilburn, who scribed a couple paranormal urban fantasy novels, *The Vampire Shrink*, and *Dark Harvest*, noticed a curious thing happening in her own private work, in real life. During their therapy sessions, many women spoke dreams of dark, fanged strangers. They told tales of nocturnal journeys into forbidden worlds where they encountered -- and became intimate with vampires. This is hardly new to readers of Martin Riccardo's *Liquid Dreams of Vampires*, he did his entire book on peoples dreams of vampires. Yet Hilbum took her listening to stories and fascinated by the vampire theme and wrote the first of many vampire books, inspired by the dreams of her clients. *The Vampire Shrink* came from a voice mail and left a message asking for referrals in another city for her daughter, who'd decided to become a vampire.

In the first novel we meet Denver Psychologist Kismet Knight. She yearns for excitement in her life, who doesn't believe in the paranormal. Her newest client pulls her into the vampire underworld, and introduces her to gorgeous Devereux the 800-year-old vampire. During this time another killer is on the lose and leaving a wake of bloodless bodies behind. Alan Stevens, an FBI profiler, warns her that vampires are very real and that one is a murderer that takes after her. While all this takes place, Kismet realizes she has feelings for both vampire and profiler.

According to publishing sources, sales of vampire romance have broken records over the past twenty years. Oddly though, vampire popularity occurred after the terrible events of September 11, 2001. "There are several theories about the increase in sales of vampire romance," Hilburn said. "A recent view is that women feel less safe and secure in the world, and the previous symbols of strong, semi-dangerous males -- our law enforcement and military warriors -- were replaced by supernatural beings. Indestructible supernatural beings. Unlike the undead, real flesh-and-blood men can be killed in war or through terrorist acts. Facing a frightening daily "reality" made escaping into magical worlds, filled with all-powerful, appealing immortals, a healthy coping mechanism....Women in therapy often report disappointment with the 'human' males they're in relationship with," Hilburn said. "Would a handsome vampire sit in front of the television, scratching his stomach and drinking beer? Are women lusting after the undead Homer Simpson? Probably not. Imagining a heart-stoppingly-gorgeous man hovering outside your window is much more fun. Most of my clients would open the window."

Some people, like Chrysie, spoke of power and despite the danger – or maybe because of it – had a need for surrender in the vampires embrace, describing the allure of vampires as this, *"It's hard to say exactly what first attracted me to vampires. I have always been fascinated by the very concept. The erotic aspect for me is the sharing itself. There are few if any more intimate acts then the sharing of blood. The idea of being powerless to stop it (in terms of the fictional side) combined with the idea of becoming permanently part of each other. There is a roguish romantic appeal to the immortal lover as well. The restrictive rules of and roles of polite society does not apply for them. They see something pleasurable they indulge it. A kind of animalistic passion with an intelligence directing it.*

Believe it or not my first exposure to Vampires comes from an old episode of Buck Rodgers (same with my fascination with Satyrs). In the episode they had a vampire like creature that would draw life force out of some one through his fingers. After that I would read anything or watch any movie or TV show that involved vampires. Historically speaking Elisabeth Bathory is the one that grabs me. Her sweetly sadistic nature just calls out to my deepest and darkest side. The one literary character that fascinates me is Marious from Anne Rice's Vampire sagas. There is something about his artistic and yet reserved nature that draws me in."

Vampire Erotica

Sara Hackenberg, an assistant professor of English at San Francisco State University, says the attraction is more basic – or base. "Vampires are pretty much always about sex." The aspect of Rice's vampires being homoerotic gets blatant in erotica books, as in stories like *Brothers of the Night: Gay Vampire Stories* by author Micheal Rowe in 1997. As the description reads, *Few objects of desire are sexier or appeal to our fantasies more than the undead, and this anthology has erotic, homosexual vampires crawling across every page. The quality of the fiction is excellent and each story burns with the kind of passion that true fans of vampiric blood lust have come to expect. A true page turner that's guaranteed to keep you up all night, one way or another.* As the Cleis Press introduction says, *cultural landscape blasted by AIDS and social alienation. Our first collection of gay vampire stories, Sons of Darkness: Tales of Men, Blood and Immortality…The vampire is queer, by definition. It is no accident that the public's fascination with vampires has always peaked at times of shifting sexuality and growing conservatism: In repressive Victorian England was born Count Dracula; the paranoid and depressed 1930s, following the decadent and sensualist 1920s, were haunted by the vampire films of Universal Pictures, and by Bela Lugosi, who will forever serve as film's defining vampire. The conservative and (in the United States) McCarthy-badgered late 1950s brought Hammer Studio's Horror of Dracula, and its many sequels rode the wave of newfound sexual permissiveness, the women's movement, lesbian and gay rights, the countercultural youth movements, and everything else that the 1960s had to offer. Now, of course, in the age of AIDS and the sex-phobia it has engendered, comes a revival of gothic culture and a widespread interest in vampires. Lesbian themes are common in contemporary horror fiction and movies. But work involving male homoeroticism is rare in horror, being largely limited to tales of gay male serial killers and psychopaths with father-fixations. Certainly this has begun to change in recent years, and books like Sons of Darkness and Brothers of the Night are certainly forging new ground, which is an intoxicating opportunity.*

Lesbian vampire erotica, not surprisingly has flown off the shelves as well from Cleis Press and others. *Love in Vein*, edited by Poppy Z. Brite; *Erotica Vampirica*, edited by Celia Tan, and the Dark Moon Press anthology *Bloody Kisses*, could all very well be acted out in film, and are simply better written that the average triple X movies. A listing of nearly every book and film I could locate on vampires is in the back of this book for quick reference.

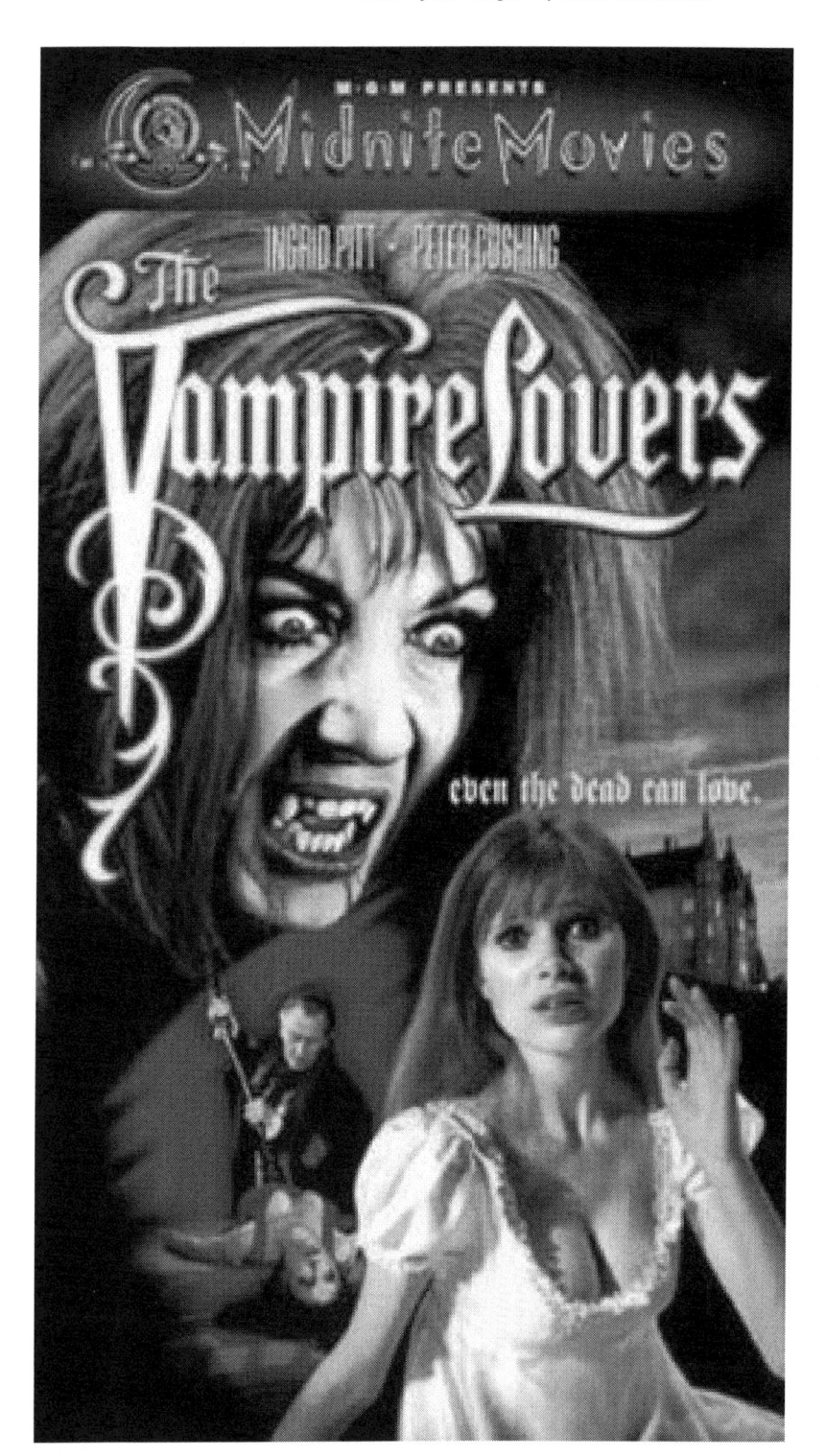

Allure of the Vampire by Corvis Nocturnum

Chapter Two

The Vampire on the Silver Screen

"Should we put out the light? And then put out the light. But once put out thy light, I cannot give it vital breath again. It needs must wither."~ Lestat, from *Interview with the Vampire*

Vampires are a reflection of the beholder, and bring out the repressed emotions of their audience as they show the heights of our hidden passions in life. Unlike other monsters that lack a humanistic visage or personality, the vampire in cinema gives us a look at ourselves, though cloaked in a predator's guise. By helping us in exploring taboo subjects in a metaphorical context, allowing situations that would normally be considered unacceptable as vampires challenge the morals of its own particular time period. Like books and poems that inspired television playwrights and modern screenplays, each eras depiction is deemed explicit when viewed during its day. To view our eras as extreme in comparison of the films of the past (short of the Adult industries depiction, of course) would be an error of narrow thinking.

Risqué indeed was the original works of Lord Byron and Palidori were performed on stage, as was *Dracula*. As technology advanced, we witnessed *Nosferatu* and *Dracula* in black and white on the silver screen. Television was no stranger to vampires, long before *Buffy* became a hit. We watch vampires because we love vampires, not because we think of them as monsters. We desire them and want them as much as they stalk us in book or played out before us in the darkened theater.

The 1897 tale *Dracula* has been turned into countless films, and in many they featured a harem of women seducing the young engaged Harker. Sexuality oozes off of Stokers original work, for example, voluptuous is an adjective used often by Stoker in his writing, and he fully revealed the lustful desires of his characters when he portrays the human women as ravenous. When speaking about *The Kama Sutra*, with in Coopla's mega successful film of Dracula by Winona Ryder's version of the character Mina, her lust is evident. As we learned last chapter, the writer, far from glorifying sex with the tale was in fact used it to equate lust with evil. Calling Lucy "carnal and unspiritual" and after her destruction as "sweetness and purity," reinforcing his puritanical preaching of feminine wiles as sinful. A vocal protestor of pornography,

Stoker used his hero Van Helsing to appear staunch defenders of purity, while destroying vampires, and that the creature Dracula forcing himself on the women was akin to rape. A far cry from how women in the audience reacted to Christopher Lee's portrayal of the same act! If ever there were a Freudian metaphor for sex is the penetration of the stake, from the orgasmic reactions the recipients, with the shaking and convulsions, to its obvious phallic shape piercing the flesh. Ironically, the Francis Cooplas' version did a one-eighty, calling the film "the strangest passion the world has ever known" and in 1992 ads printed saying "Love never dies." His famous screen version instead as the "repressed Victorian sexuality" an aspect he focused on this quite heavily. Stoker would not have been pleased. Long before Coopla, Lugosi commented on thousands of love letters from women, whose ages ranged from seventeen to thirty years old, and the same thing happening to Christopher Lee when he took the role. Gary Oldman spoke of him as a tortured soul, trying to play him as a fallen angel. Still others today look to vampires as role models. In fact, a friend of mine by the name of Kelvin commented on Stoker's character:

The eroticism of the vampire is one thing I did not understand until I matured when I learned more about sexuality and sensuality, and that is the vampire's perfect weapons when it comes to the art of seduction. My fascination with the vampire evolved over the years after

Allure of the Vampire by Corvis Nocturnum

Dracula because he has taught me to be a gentleman and fight back when I was attacked by foolish people. Vlad Tepes Dracula (The real warlord) is an evocation of understanding on what kind of man Dracula is. Dracula was a hero to some people and a monster to the cowardly ingrates who did not understood him. At long last, Dracula is seen as for more than the villain Stoker painted. Taking the sexuality of Camilla and Stoker to more obvious heights in film was the 1970s movie *The Vampire Lovers*, and *The Contess*, roughly patterned after Bathory. Subtle homosexual undertones hinted at in *Interview with a Vampire* grew over time to outright pornography in other movies, such as that in *Les Vampires*. In all of them, the dark sensuality and allure combines sadomasochism and blood with nudity to heighten excitement. This makes it appealing to any gender or sexual orientation. The before mentioned books became movies, thrilling the newcomers, and for the most part, the die hard book lovers, who, with some exceptions felt some films were not true enough to the original novels. In a 1979 vampire film starring a major heart throb from the early days of classic films....*had a wonderful cast including Sir Laurence Olivier. Women of all ages were packing theatres to see this hot sexy vampire version. I can remember women saying they left their hubbies home so they wouldn't see them swoon... Many put the film right up there with Bela Lagossi for "early vamp hotness"*. I would hazard to say that this was the first time in decades that the vampire genre climbed back out of the pit of *drive-in, late night schlock and retook it place in cinema as a genre worthy of respect and notable box office attention... truly a guilty pleasure for adult women of that time,* says Lenore.

The Nude Vampire

In this old classic, Pierre Radamante (Olivier Martin) happens upon a beautiful young woman wearing nothing but a sheer orange gown running down a dark street one night, he finds himself attacked by men wearing ominous animal masks. The assailants shoot and capture the girl (played by Caroline Cartier), but Pierre manages to escape. Determined to discover the cause, he breaks into the secret club in very much similar to the one in Stanley Kubrick's film, *Eyes Wide Shut,* discovering a 'suicide cult' that worships the girl, who is alive unharmed. Pierre discovers she's a prisoner of his depraved father (Maurice Lemaître), an eccentric millionaire, who believes she's a vampire. As we see in a hidden laboratory Pierre's father uses the girl to find immortality. In his efforts to rescue her, Pierre has to contend with his father scientists, the cult, and a secret society of dimension jumpers.

Director Jean Rollin's first film, 1967's *Rape Of The Vampire*, caused such an uproar audiences shouted and threw trash at the screen. French critics came up with the term 'Rollinade' to describe films which they deemed amateurish, and nonsensical, yet today a great many fans around the world are certainly pleased he pushed onward despite naysayers. *The Nude Vampire* was Rollin's second feature-length film (and first color film.) *Requiem For A Vampire, Le Frisson des Vampires* all make use of lighting and shadows in eerie, cold, black and white, reflecting back on his penchant for early German expressionist cinema (like *Nosferatu*) and classic American horror. Rollin's work depicted his vampires classical, with coffins, crypts and bare breasts., with the likes of Caroline Cartier portrays the naked vampire and the twins are played by real-life twins Catherine Castel in *Lips of Blood*, and *Bacchanales Sexuelles* and Marie-Pierre Castel from *Requiem For A Vampire* and *Le Frisson des Vampires*.

Hammer films

Most progressive in the early days of silver screen was Hammer Films, founded in 1934. Between 1950 until the mid 1970's they quickly became a powerhouse among horror movies, utilizing British actors and actresses in the roles. Many of the vampire themed flicks starred Polish actress Ingrid Pitt as the villainess, who created memorable iconic images for the femme fatal. Hypocritically, these British gay-paranoid films of the 1960s and 1970s are often noted for blatant feminine sexuality, the rivalry and seduction between Dracula and his male foes becomes unequivocally homoerotic. As much as Hammer films represented the fear of homosexuality in their subtext, they blatantly represented its desire in the slew of exploitive lesbian vampire films in the *Karnstein Trilogy* comprises of *The Vampire Lovers*, *Lust for a Vampire*, and *Twins of Evil* all based loosely on the early vampire novel *Carmilla*.

Without such works as Hammer produced, we would not have the popular female version of this icon in film and art we see today.

The Satanic Rites of Dracula in 1972 starring Christopher Lee started the trend away from the romantic settings in favor of a more modern approach. Critics did not care for the movie nor did Lee himself, who refused to appear in anymore Dracula films Afterwords. At a press conference in 1973 on *The Satanic Rites of Dracula*, then renamed *Dracula is Dead... and Well and Living in London,* Lee said: *"I'm doing it under protest... I think it is fatuous. I can think of twenty adjectives - fatuous, pointless, absurd. It's not a comedy, but it's got a comic title. I don't see the point."*

Vampira

Television's original horror-show hostess, born Maila Nurmi, played Vampira. Thin 'Morticia Addams' lady had fans all over the world at the height of her fame in the mid-'50s, when her show aired on L.A.'s KABC. One of her fans was director Ed Wood, who cast her in 1956 for his no-budget horror and attained new heights of fame through Tim

Burton's efforts. She was a popular pinup model for the artist Vargas, but KABC canceled her show in 1955. "There was a horror craze going on," she recalled once, "and I was thinking someone was going to knock on my door. Mr. Wood did. I was on unemployment-$13 a week-and I was paid $200 for one day.'" In the late 1950s and early 1960s she made three movies then later in the mid-60s she opened a clothing boutique called Vampira's Attic.

Elvira, sex siren

Many fans of vampires stem from low-budget films, like Cindi, who mention *Dark Shadow*s as her earliest recollection of being enamored with vampires, "the cheesy B-rated horror programs, like Sir Graves and Elvira." Elvira's real name is Cassandra Peterson, but called herself the Mistress of the Dark in her self-titled B horror movies and on her late-night cult and horror movie. She moved to Las Vegas, immediately after graduating high school. She showcased her talents singing and dancing; and eventually meets Elvis Presley. Taking his encouraging advice on being a performer she joined an Italian rock band and toured as their lead singer.

It is a little known fact that at the young age of five, she tipped a pot of boiling water over onto herself.

After undergoing numerous skin grafts and covered her scars. The dress she wore as Elvira only exposed the parts of her skin that were not damaged. Determinedly, Peterson found fame wearing a black, gothic, cleavage-enhancing gown as host of *Movie Macabre*, a weekly horror movie presentation. Her wicked look was countered by her attitude, a quick-witted personality. Producers began bringing the show back, producers asked Nurmi to revive *The Vampira Show*. Nurmi herself had worked on the project for a short time, but eventually quit. The station continued and sent out a casting call. Cassandra auditioned against 200 other horror hostess hopefuls, and won the role. They allowed her to create Elvira's image. Before the first taping, producers received a cease and desist letter from Nurmi. Unable to continue with the Vampira character, the name Elvira created. Elvira character rapidly gained notoriety with her tight fitting, low cut black showing more cleavage than had ever appeared on television before. She reclined on a red Victorian couch, introducing the movie commenting on the often travesty of film that came next. She used risque double entendres made frequent jokes about her eye-popping cleavage. In an AOL Entertainment News interview, Peterson revealed, "I figured out that Elvira is me when I was a teenager. She's a spastic girl. I just say what I feel and people seem to enjoy it." The then emerging Goth subculture caused a demand for Elvira throughout the Eighties. A frequent guest on many talk shows, she also produced a long series of Halloween-themed ads and guest roles on television dramas such as *CHiPS*, *The Fall Guy*, and on numerous awards shows as a presenter. However, Peterson has always been reluctant to appear in television interviews and specials as herself. She has been offered to do a *Playboy* spread as Elvira, but declined. However, she has done a shoot for them as herself.

She's appeared on the cover of *Femme Fatales* magazine five times. Her popularity reached its zenith with the release of the feature film, *Elvira, Mistress of the Dark* which she co-wrote in 1988.

Red Vamp

Red Vamp is an established gothic personality and model. Now an up-and-coming classic horror hostess for the show, currently airing on ScreamTV.net called "Red Vamp's Classic Tales of Horror," that features classic horror movies from the 1920's-1960's, such as those showcasing the great horror icons of Bela Lugosi, Lon Chaney, Boris Karloff, and Vincent Price. She introduces and concludes each movie with info, trivia and comments on each film, such as *Nosferatu*, *Dr. Jekyll & Mr. Hyde*, *Dementia 13*, and *The Cabinet of Dr. Caligari* are examples of films featured on the show. One can still see episodes typically air Friday nights at 7PM Central and stream worldwide, however the schedule varies and current broadcast times must be checked on the *ScreamTV.net* website.

She's been referred to as "this generation's Elvira" by several significantly famous individuals such as Bela Lugosi Jr., who referred to her as Cassandra Peterson's rival. Red Vamp has made appearances at conventions, alongside people such as Bela Lugosi Jr. (only child of Bela Sr.), Sarah

Photo courtesy of Red Vamp

Karloff (daughter of Boris Karloff), Ron Chaney (grandson of Lon Chany Jr., great-grandson of Lon Chaney), the cast of the original Creature from the Black Lagoon, as well as many others.

She has had her share of public appearances and those on television and online. "*I started working with After Dark Jewelry through knowing other people who model for them, Natasha Frost, the owner, designs very dark, beautiful jewelry that is perfect for my style and for the clothing that I wear on Red Vamp's Classic Tales of Horror. The jewelry is very fitting of the gothic and horror type modeling appearances*". She explained she has been a model previously, saying, "*I am very particular about the type of modeling, the project involved, etc. I am always open to new projects and opportunities, but it does have to fit largely within my own standards, tastes…I would love to be able to go forward with horror hosting and other similar projects using the Red Vamp persona. However, my true goals always lie within my family. I believe the true measure of success is having a strong and happy personal life with family, marriage, etc. So, what is always most important to me is keeping my first priority my family and enjoying each and every day with them. I would love to achieve even 1/10th the success that someone such as Elvira has achieved, but any career success that may come alongside a happy personal life is only icing on the cake. In addition, it is important to me to use any success for positive causes, such as support for March of Dimes, Autism Research and Animal Rescue/Adoption."*

This stunning lady holds several other credits to her name, as a cover model for *Bite Me!* and *Gothic Beauty* magazines, appearances in *Dark Realms* and *CineFan Magazine* as well as a model for the After Dark Jewelry, Madame LeGoth and Amira clothing lines. Her image has been used for flyers, internet ads and been the spokesmodel for Darkness Against Domestic Violence (DADV) also known as "Shelter for Darkness plus a vast amount of artists works. A graduate from the University of North Texas, with a B.A. Psychology 2002 – Cum Laude., several acting workshops and University of North Texas Performance, Baytown Little Theater.

Lilith in film

Lilith once again resurfaced in modern times. Her name was the name of the vampiress hit woman in Jake West 1998 movie, *Razorblade Smile*, which had a lesbian scene in it as well, depicting the lead vampiress as an extremely curvy femme fatale showing her figure to obviously titillate the male viewer. Lilith is also used in films such as *Tales from the Crypt Bordello of Blood* starring Angie Everheart as the redheaded ringleader of a group of prostitutes. Interestingly she was portrayed as vampire, snake, and seductress, weaving all the myths of her into one character depiction. We see her as the mother/leader of all the creatures in Marvel comic's army fighting Nightstalkers, and in many other works of fiction. C.S. Lewis's *The Lion, the Witch and the Wardrobe*, the central antagonist, the White Witch, is said to be a descendant of Lilith. Lilith is the mother of the vampire heroine Vampirella in the comic book series, which became a movie. Lilith was also in a Gary Bussey film as he played a crazed vampire hunter in a low budget movie. In the role-playing game *Vampire: The Masquerade*, Lilith is said to be cursed by God for her insubordination and thus became the first witch, who passed her knowledge to Cain, the first vampire. *Daughters of Lilith: Women Vampires in Popular Literature* used Lilith in the title of this erotica book.

Not everyone I spoke to have explained their first love affair with vampires was during the days of mega hits of today like *Twilight* and Anne Rice. Others, like Jodie, spoke of older classics and vintage film, *"Vampires, ghosts, and the macabre were a very large part of my childhood. I can remember late night conversations with my mother and sister, the three of us sitting at the kitchen table by candlelight, discussing topics that most would find strange and unbelievable. Our house was haunted and we would 'compare notes' on what each felt, saw or heard recently. Deceased relatives would often stop by and make themselves known, especially to me, and on occasion I was given messages to relay.*

My Sunday-school teacher mother was an avid horror movie and novel enthusiast. Séances and playing with the Ouija board were pastimes in our house, Halloween was very much THE event, and our dining room bookcase was full of H.P. Lovecraft, Stephen King and

Poe. At a very young age I was more than familiar with Boris Karloff, Lon Chaney Jr. and Sr., Peter Lorre, Peter Cushing, Vincent Price, Bela Lugosi and Christopher Lee. This was partly due to Chiller Theater, a campy and completely scary (to a six year old) TV program which ran from 1963-1983 on WIIC Channel 11 in Pittsburgh. The host of the show was Bill Cardille "Chilly Billy," who you may recognize as the reporter at the end of Night of the Living Dead. Saturday nights Mom would put us to bed at our usual time of 9PM, wake us up a few hours later, and we would be up the rest of the night eating pizza while watching horror, sci-fi and fantasy movies through our fingers.

Though as a child I loved zombies and mummies, vampires always held a particular fascination for me. I often cheered for the vampire and felt it completely unfair the Count was killed just because he loved the girl. He was more powerful and passionate than any other man and would do anything to be with her. He was very much a pale knight in my eyes.

My innocent empathy lasted only so long. Soon I became aware of the physical, emotional and psychic seduction vampires embodied. Desire withstanding the ages, to exist but not have life, to love and obsess, to be both the drug and the addict.... All are concepts that strike a chord deep inside me. Often I feel a kinship of sorts with others who can understand the implications, as if a fine strand of spider's silk connects us and all it would take is a gentle tug to confirm the bond."

Barnabas Collins

television series from 1966 to 1971 known as *Dark Shadows* became a major influence on the vampire persona and our attraction to it. There were over 1,200 episodes of this soap that featured gothic horror staples like vampires, monsters, witches, werewolves, ghosts and zombies. The show has a continuing rabid fan base that populates *Dark Shadows Festival* conventions. A year into this late evening show the visiting relative, Barnabas, appears. He was freed from a chained coffin by accident and over the duration of the series he sought a cure for his disease, after an affair with a witch who enraged by his lack of interest sent a bat to infect him. He dates and preys on women, yet is remorseful about doing so. Barnabas wishes to become human again and seeks help from a medical professional. Out of pity or acknowledgement that he felt connection to humanity still, his plight and demeanor won droves of fans for the character. As a sympathetic lonely figure adapted our views on the type casting of a vampire, it affected many creations later on. To this day, fans of the show and the Collins character are still devoted. A fan of the show, Cindi, commented to me how she became hooked on vampires around this time, and said *"I'm gonna show my age here with two words - Dark Shadows! I really think that vampire was my first love. Slut that I used to be, I'm not sure*

I remember his name; was it Barnabas?" I asked about her reasoning and she replied, *"They are forbidden fruit. They tend to be flawlessly beautiful. They have seen things we can only read about in history books, which is a flawed and biased viewpoint, in my opinion. They are strong; if your boyfriend is a vampire, nobody is going to hurt you. They will outlive you, so you will never be alone. All that experience had made them aware of what makes humans human, and tolerant of the above. They are financially stable, thus good providers. To be politically incorrect, they are everything women instinctively, if subconsciously, seek in men. And if they're not (thinking of that hottie, Lucious Lestat, here), they've had many many lifetimes to perfect faking it".*

Hence the sexual prowess is confirmed, at least judging by fiction and television, to fuel the fantasies of women for centuries. As the founder of The Lost Children of Oubliette recalls, *"I was a very young child, 3 or 4 years old to start. While other children spent their afternoons sitting glued in front of the television, cuddled up with their teddy bears watching cartoons, I was hidden away in the dark of my parents heavily draped bedroom, watching Dark Shadows, curled up on top of my mothers cedar chest, imagining it to be my coffin. I was never afraid but rather longed for a world to which I could relate and to which I wanted to be a part. My Barbie dolls were re-named Barnabas, Angelique, Sara, Quentin, etc. Other children (and their parents) thought me strange and a little bit scary. I even wandered in the small cemetery across the street from my home. That was my playground. I was very quiet and tended to keep to myself".*

Numerous TV revivals of the series and adaptations have been attempted over the years. As of this writing, the actor Johnny Depp is to play Barnabas in a movie adaptation of this classic show. Warner Bros. recently closed a deal with the estate of Dan Curtis, the producer and director who created the soap that aired weekdays on ABC. Johhny Depp has said in interviews that he has always been obsessed with *Dark Shadows* and had, as a child, wanted to be Barnabas Collins. He is to co - produce with David Kennedy.

The Hunger

David Bowie left his mark with Catherine Deneuve in the movie *The Hunger*. The first important homosexual vampire film was Roy Ward Bake's *The Vampire Lovers (1970)*, an adaptation of J. Sheridan Le Fanu's *Carmilla*. Other gay vampires appeared simultaneously in Roman Polanski's *The Fearless Vampire Killers (1967)*, Lancer Brooks' *Sons of Satan (1973)*, Ulli Lommel's *Tenderness of Wolves (1973)*, and *Jimmy Sangster's Lust for a Vampire (1973)*. The concept of vampire and homosexual grew throughout the 1970s, becoming more apparent in Tony Scott's *The Hunger* when it came out in 1983. The monsters of horror films were now much more telling as a reflection of societal views, some good, and unfortunately some bad. While Anne Rice was penning more of her series, homosexuals were – and to some still are - seen as predatory, amoral, perverse, and threatening "normal" peoples life. This movie used classical music, and a very visual storytelling, presenting a sexy tale of blood, lust, and took vampires to the new level. Susan Sarandon is attempting to discover the secrets of natural aging. Both of the lead vampire characters played by Bowie and Deneuve meet a tragic end, as Bowie finds himself rotting away, slowly. Once Bowie is out of the picture, Deneuve has her sights on Sarandon and we see a love scene between them. This writing is masterfully done as a tragic drama, the writers made a hit with the *Bela Lugosi Is Dead* opening, easily making this a classic.

Buffy

Ever since the Spike and Buffy implied fellatio scene, its popularity soared. Perhaps this was just because of the mildly shocking scene but then again maybe because there were marked similarities to the trio of femme fatales with Jonathan Harker who offered the same pleasurable act. The reinforcement of oral fixation with vampires and eroticism will continue to be speculated on by psychologists and writers alike.

In the relationship they have, Buffy and Spike depict frequent fights which ever increasingly become more and more sexual. When at last Spike says to Buffy that he loves her, she reacts violently, saying "I do beat him up a lot. For him, that's like third base" Symbolically we see near foreplay in their first sexual encounter is a knock-down fight, as Spike tells her, "I wasn't planning to hurt you. Much," right before she lands a blow, then kisses him to commence yet another blow! They, in their twisted relationship portray a fitting climax to a series *Dying for a kiss* was more than an expression for Spike.

Death and sex tied to vampires evolves even more as Buffy continues with Angel. There was a twist on the vampire mythos after their first kiss in season one and this is the only incident where a vampire's transformation occurs in such manner. Sexual arousal is the catalyst in the change, but it does contain a Freudian style oral eroticism just as powerful as any displayed in Stoker's *Dracula*. Hopelessly, Buffy wishes to deny the truth that she can't remain an innocent and save the world, and as she can't remain sexually innocent forever.

J. Gordon Melton gave a lecture on religion and vampires stating, "Parodies ranging from the genuinely humorous to tasteless pornography have already appeared." He goes on to say, "In the mundane world of everyday existence, vampirism, at best, is a psychological/sociological metaphor with some limited utility in highlighting elements of human sexuality and unbalanced personal power-relationships." I couldn't agree more with Melton, as my research kept proving the we as people continue to slightly adjust the vampire to fit our own sexuality as a species, yet pushing the envelope ever so slightly every time.

Once Bitten

The virginal and purity violated by a vampire switches from male to female with one of Jim Carrey's early works from 1985. The conquest of a master vampire violating or corruption the innocent is a victory of power in this spoof, as a young Carrey is seduced by a beautiful older woman who spans the ages to snare virgin males to keep herself alive. A nod perhaps to Countess Bathory, yet it still retains old fashioned ideals, seemingly confirming the notion that sex acts are immoral outside of marriage.

The Countess in this movie is a 400 year old vampire who will cease to look young unless she is able to feed on a virgin three times before Halloween, which is a week away. She sends Sebastian, her servant and all of her lesser vampires out to locate one. Carrey's character, Mark has a problem of his own, and is, ironically, just the opposite issue. He wants to 'do it' as he so eloquently puts it, with Robin, his girlfriend, however she wants to wait. Teenage hormones meets a role reversal in the vampire hot after a young human female, as Jamie and Russ, Mark's equally immature friends convince him to go to a Hollywood pick up spot where Mark meets the Countess, on the prowl. As the story finishes, we see Mark saved by losing his virginity in a coffin the Countess home.

Lost Boys

Vampires as rough and urban teens is a far cry from the days of Lugosi. The paranoia and ugliness surrounding the 1980s vampire film is often linked to reflecting the public fear of homosexual culture and AIDS. We see sexuality in these films was heightened yet again, but the films were bleak over all. Following the divorce of their parents, Michael, played by Jason Patric and Sam, played by Corey Haim in his most famous role, along with their mother Lucy, Dianne Wiest, move to Santa Carla, California to live with their mother's father, a peculiar old man. Santa Carla happens to be the murder capital of the world. Santa Carla is a beach town with a boardwalk and the kids that hang out there, including a group of tough kids lead by David, played by Keifer Sutherland. While Lucy gets a job working for Max [Edward Herrmann] at the local video store, Sam befriends the Frog Brothers, Edgar (Corey Feldman) and Alan (Jamison Newlander) who inform Sam that Santa Carla is crawling with vampires.

Meanwhile, Michael becomes enthralled by the mysterious female vampire Star, who happens to be the girlfriend of David. The gang takes Michael to their hideout, and Michael inadvertently drinks David's blood, thinking it is wine. Michael develops vampire traits sensitivity to sounds, a lack of reflection, and even flying. Sam accuses Michael of being a vampire but Michael convinces Sam that he can figure out how to fix it. Instead, Michael sleeps with Star. Sam decides to take matters into his own hands and asks for counsel from the Frog Brothers who promptly tell Sam that the only remedy is to drive a stake in Michael's heart but that Michael may only be a half-vampire, in which case, if the head vampire is killed, Michael will go back to normal.

Forever Knight

Like Barnabas Collins of *Dark Shadows*, the killer vampire turned police detective Nick Knight also sought to return to his previous human state with the help of someone in medicine. This 1989 movie on CBS starring Rick Springfield became a 1992 television series with Geraint Wyn Davies as the lead.

Natalie Lambert, played by Deborah Duchene, Nick's friend and love interest (albeit one-sided on her part) is the city medical examiner who continually tries to wean Nick off blood. Emotionally charged episodes show Nick lose both human and century old friends, making him appealing to fans as a caring sensitive victim of a rash choice ages ago. Using his abilities to fight crime and balance the scales of all his misdeeds people found a vampire much like themselves. He hopes to find his mortality and yet he is at odds with his vampire family to whom he is tied. Nick has a bit of a love triangle going on with Natalie and Janette because he has ages of shared history with her and bonded with her. Whenever Nick displayed his urges around women his fangs grew which he did his best to hide. One cannot help but be struck by the phallic image of both the piercing ability and extension, commonly seen in countless vampire scenes, but specifically in this series it is focused on by the camera work. Even the actors themselves talked about sexuality during a chat room interview between Nigel Bennet, Geraint Wyn Davies, and producer Jim Parriott. Mr. Parriott said, "It's penetration. I mean fang penetration. It's unrequited love. You know, vampires can't actually do it without killing the woman, so there's a whole tension there." Geraint (Nick Knight) added, "But also, for the woman or the person being brought over, it is the ultimate act of submission. You are giving your life, you're not just giving your body, but your whole being to this entity, this vampire.

Nigel (Lacroix) suggested his thinking on it by saying, "It's all the stuff that leads up to it that's romantic." The producer said, "I think that the whole idea of unrequited love, if I may repeat myself, I think that's the whole deal. It's romantic. You can have that. But, it doesn't end in sex. It can't end in sex with a vampire. So, there's a whole tension there, and that is good." Geraint summed up by saying, "And also, the man or the vampire brings centuries of history and of lovemaking. I mean, there is a skill there, a huge skill, which is sexy and which is romantic. And, other than the feeding frenzy which people put into vampire lore, it is incredibly sensual as well as sexual."

The idea of human mortality and connection blurring in the after 'life' of vampires is brought out as Nick and Janette's creator Lacroix (Nigel Bennett) reveals his past. Lacroix was a general in the Roman army who returned to Divia his pre-teen daughter, formerly ill, but now healthy who embraces him telling him he can live forever. Father and daughter travel to Egypt and in the tomb of her maker, Qa'Ra an ancient vampire. The daughter attempts to seduce Lacroix who decapitates her.

Later Divia returns to kill her father, but then decides to murder Nick because of the attachment he has for Nick as a son. Taunting Lacroix, she distracts him to slay him but Nick rushes in and saves his mentor.

By the end of the series Natalie requests Nick turn her in order to live forever with him, but he is afraid of draining her unto death. He agrees but cannot stop himself, overcome with memories, Lacroix shows up and says turn her or kill her. Nick, overcome with the guilt of subjecting her to an eternity of darkness he hands Lacroix a stake. His 'father' says life is a gift and asks Nick if his faith makes him think there is light at the end of the tunnel. Unable to answer he replies he will know when he dies. Nick is shown kneeling next to Natalie and Lacroix raises the stake screaming "Damn you Nicholas" furious at Nick's choice to end his life. We are left to think both Nick and Natalie die, ending the series much more dark than the first two seasons showed. However, as the producer said, "We didn't end it. We left the final frame on Lacroix with his stake raised. We never saw it come down." Perhaps Nick still continues to prowl the streets, as he does in the mind of the fans to this day.

The Vampire Chronicles

Perhaps the most obvious and widespread vampire on film to present itself as sexual, as far as male vampires go, are those of Anne Rice chronicles. The director of *Interview with the Vampire* in 1994 stated Rice's creations were "a combination between the angel Gabriel and Bela Lugosi." Outcasts, especially in the Goth communities had already used vampirish appearance and sorrowful demeanor due to the fact the vibe deeply felt in the first book turned film was of that of bitter loneliness and isolation. The adoring fans felt a kinship, and so these Byronic rebels' attitude and attire did much to heighten the mystique. Louis shifts his attention for Claudia to Armand, and his tone when speaking to the reporter, touching seems to straddle the line between eroticism and fear. The gay community fell in love with the series, as did women, when Rice brought the vampire out of the coffin – or closet. Rice herself contributed to the awareness of the problem AIDS in the 1980's as she had a fondness for the homosexual crowds in San Francisco. The excessiveness of vampires, the decadence they exuded was easily linked to similar mannerisms used by her friends. Lestat has the attitude in the first book and as he evolved in the following books, he does so in a similar as the courage she saw in the gays facing prejudice of people during her era. Most of us now see gay as the norm, almost to the point of metro sexual or the token gay person in a show on television as the norm, at one time it would have shocked the world. I see a comparison in the fiction of vampires evolving in a more obvious way in the 1980's to now, but it has always been an undercurrent since *Carmilla*. People who study vampires and gay lifestyle will attest to the fact each has its subtle mannerisms, language, and a forbidden world residing under the noses of those who would ignore it if even faced with its repellent perversions. Rice commented that the marble statues very much seemed androgynous, the old world of her vampires had similar qualities, a fact implied in so many cemetery scenes in her books and the films eerie sets. Further, Rice showed her contempt in the mainstream for *Queen of the Dammed,* who in causing atrocities in cases such as the Nazis holocaust (homophobia taken to its monstrous proportional scale) and used Akashas contempt for most of man – the root of all evil who was destroyed in her lusts for destruction. According to Katherine Ramesland's book with Rice, she was attempting to show an image of AIDS devastation on the gay community as well. In her world, the victim is the powerful seducer and destroyer of life, yet offers the Dark Gift to those worthy of it.

It's important to note that gay families struggling with matters of acceptance in 1976, challenged the traditional family structure decades before our current debates on the legal and morality fights over gay marriage It also seems to portray a dysfunctional family. Both, for example, can be seen herein the adaptation of Rice's first movie from *The Vampire Chronicles, Interview with the Vampire.* In an attempt to keep Louis from leaving him Lestat gives a child, Claudia, the "dark gift" after Louis has fed upon her. Lestat explains their new 'family'.

'Now Louis was going to leave us,' said Lestat, his eyes moving from my face to hers. 'He was going to go away. But now he's not.

Because he wants to stay and take care of you and make you happy.' He looked at me. 'You're not going, are you Louis?' 'You bastard!' I whispered to him, 'You fiend! "Such language in front of your daughter,' he said.

Vampire in Brooklyn

One normally doesn't think of actor Eddie Murphy as a vampire, yet in 1995 Wes Craven's *Vampire in Brooklyn* was released. This horror comedy had its moments of almost too tongue in cheek, yet for the most part I felt the chemistry between Eddie's character Maximillian and Angela Bassett was very strong.

Wes Craven directed this cult classic and portrayed the inner conflict of power and seduction. Throughout the film, Max offers her things beyond her wildest dreams, invading her nightmares. Although he is killed before she permanently is turned into a full blooded vampire it leaves many lingering moral and ethical quandaries that I enjoyed.

Embrace of the Vampire

I'd have to agree with an online review I ran across talking about *Embrace of the Vampire*. This is one of the most famous B movies ever filmed because of a few key nude scenes; not because of a good storyline or depiction of the vampire. Alyssa Milano looks great, in this 1995 flick, but that doesn't mean that this was a good movie. In this movie the writers clearly were more concerned with getting Alyssa naked than making a piece of art. The only thing realistic presented is that it comes from the view of a young college girl set on experiencing life for the first time on her own. We find in the film that the vampire stalking her believes she is the reincarnation of his wife who never could cope with her death. Similar to Coopla's version of *Dracula*, in idea only not by any means the quality of the epic, this Count returns home from the Crusades to find his beloved wife had killed herself on the false rumors of his death. Then much later, he begins to pursue and seduce her in modern day. The rest is her inner struggle where she faces erotic dreams, voices, seduction, mixed with the anxiety of many young people who leave the familiarity of home to go on to college, complete with multiple erotic legendary soft-porn lesbian scenes. The initial lesbian scene with Melissa Milano and Charlotte Lewis not only is appealing to a voyeuristic audience, but real in the sense of portraying a nervous young woman in a same sex encounter for the first time.

From Dusk Till Dawn

Who could ever forget the scene in which Selma Hayek appeared with a group of strippers in *From Dusk till Dawn*, complete with coiled snake? The Gecko Brothers, Seth played by George Clooney and Richie played by Quentin Tarantino, are on a crime spree in the first of a trilogy starting with this 1996 vampire flick, directed by Tarantino. First stop is a bank in Abilene, Texas, where they kill four Texas rangers and a civilian, take a bank teller as hostage, and head for the Mexican border. Afterwards they hit Benny's World of Liquor, where they kill the shopkeeper, a sheriff, and burn down the building. Their final stop is the Dew Drop Motel where Richie kills the hostage, Seth arranges with Carlos, played by Cheech Marin, for sanctuary in El Rey. The brothers kidnap Pastor Jake Fuller (Harvey Keitel), his two kids Kate and Scott. Commandeering their RV, the killer head for the Titty Twister bar where they are to rendezvous with Carlos. The Titty Twister turns out to be a vampire bar, and before long dinner is served. The vampires start biting the humans and the humans staking the vampires, until only Seth and Kate are left. Just at the stroke of dawn, Carlos shows up and opens the door, letting in the morning sun. Kate goes back home and Seth goes on to El Rey.

Kindred: The Embraced

A favorite of mine from some time back is *Kindred: The Embraced* premiered on Fox television on April 2, 1996 produced by *John Leekley Productions* and *Spelling Television*. The show was loved by a small but loyal following, loosely based on the popular role-playing game *Vampire: The Masquerade*. The series focused on a San Franciscan police detective Frank Kohanek, played by C. Thomas Howell, who discovers his city is home to numerous vampires while investigating alleged mobster, Julian Luna, who is played by Mark Frankel. Julian Luna, prince of several disparate vampire or kindred clans in San Francisco, tried to keep a tenuous peace among them while applying ruthless justice against those who broke the rules. Infractions that merit "final death" as it is called when they kill one of their own include the taking of human life and changing humans into vampires who have not volunteered for the transformation. The vampires survive through the masquerade, disguising themselves as humans, while Julian strictly enforces the laws that govern them in order to protect their anonymity. The two form an uneasy bond with one another as they work together to try to prevent a vampire war and Julian struggles with his romantic feelings for a human reporter Caitlin Byrne, played by Kelly Rutherford.

This series ran for eight episodes ahead of the conclusion of the first season on May 9, 1996 before it was canceled. Later it was released on a two volume DVD box set on August 21, 2001. *Sci Fi Weekly's* Kathie Huddleston called praised the character of Julian as a "multifaceted character who's both good and evil".

John Carpenter's Vampires

In 1998 John Carpenter's Vampires tells of vampire-hunters deployed by the Vatican led by Jack Crow, to hunt down and destroy the vampires before they find a crucifix. Together with his only living colleague Tony Montoya, Katrina, a hooker who will turn into a vampire soon, and a newly assigned and inexperienced priest named Father Adam Guitea, Crow sets out to find the black cross first. If they fail, vampires will be able to walk in the sun. What intrigued me about the vampire here and sexuality is that Valek, the master vampire is shown mesmerizing and performing the bite on one of the main characters, Katrina, in a suggestive manner when he disappears of screen but we clearly see the orgasmic face of his victim. Of course, she and others are shown naked in a few parts of the film; especially when of Jack's team gets taken out in revenge during a drunken orgy in a sleazy motel. Violence, blood and sex, oh my, a teenagers best combination – but seriously, I do count it as a favorite of mine, in part because Valek just looks too cool in his all black flowing long coat.

We hear a bit of low brow humor between Jack and Father Guiteau during the following dialog:

Jack: Let me ask you a question.
When you were stabbing that vampire, did you get a little wood?
Father: Mahogany.
Jack: Excuse me?
Father: Ebony. Teak!
Jack: Are you possessed by demons?
Father: A major chubby.
Jack: Language, Padre.

Of course, it may be love or vampire gaze, but two 'normal' vampires, Jack's partner Montoya and Katrina do add a bit of touching drama, in my humble opinion.

BloodRayne

In the movie *BloodRayne* Kristanna Loken stars as the main character, Rayne, the half human, half vampire (known as a Dhampir) hunter based off the popular video game of the same name. This flick is definitely geared toward the young (and older) male viewers/video game players whom, it is assumed, will enjoy the scantily clad main character but over all it was a fairly low budget film. It was of better quality than *Vampirella* by far but not particularly noteworthy overall. There were several notable actors and actresses involved in the making of this film such as Michelle Rodriguez, Ben

Kingsley, Meatloaf, Udo Kier, Billy Zane and Michael Madsen.

Van Helsing

In a far cry from Stokers original character we see a younger version of Van Helsing played by Hugh Jackman as a gun toting rebel fighting everything from Hyde to Dracula. He retains his hero status as the angel Gabriel, but is suffering from amnesia. As a child adopted and raised to battle evil by the Church, he is depicted in this CGI laden action film has him waging war on Dracula. This Count changed in quite an unusual way from the typical, as he and his trio of wives were attempting to populate the world with their own children, not by embracing humans. I note that all three of wore tattered and revealing gowns, as sultry as ever where those in Stokers tale seducing Jonathan Harker. There is a heartfelt moment in the end when Jackman's character is holding his dying love but I still can't help but feel Dracula and his brides in this movie were the victims after all. Other than that, it's a fairly simple yet compelling tale, paying homage to classic horror movies of yesterday in certain places.

Underworld

This action trilogy of vampire films, done in the year 2003, 2006 and 2009 are all my personal favorites, what with its slick outfits, ranging from various themes and types of vampires, such as antiquity to tight latex and leather, to guns a blazing, and absolutely gorgeous Gothic settings. Things heat up quickly in the romance between the two central characters, as Selene, played by Kate Beckinsale, a vampire Death dealer, reluctantly falls for the half vampire half werewolf character Micheal, played by Scott Speedman. The story in *Underworld Evolution* continues from the same night as the end of the first movie, and shows a rather graphic lovemaking sequence. Almost in a Romeo and Juliet styled tragedy, the pair have a forbidden love, as the hybrid started out as simply a werewolf. Given the fact the Lycans, as they are called, are in an all out war with the vampires for centuries, it matters little to either side that Selene bites him and alters his DNA to be a predator more powerful than either species.

Vampire sexuality becomes overt

The 1970s should have been called the Golden Age of lesbian vampire movies. Among the many examples are *Vampyros Lesbos, Daughters of Darkness,* and *The Velvet Vampire.* These films established the image of the female vampire as a ravishing seductress. Filmmaker Andrea Weiss says that the lesbian vampire represents the threat posed by feminism. This era also saw the emergence of the campy vampire.

Blacula in 1972 was about two gay antique collectors awaking a vampire who was once a African prince, and Andy Warhol's *Blood for Dracula* (1974), depicted a vampire who must feed on virgins, yet can only find prostitutes. As we look at the movies and indeed, our cable television, it is clear it is an ongoing trend.

The Insatiable

The year 2006 gave us a great film in *The Insatiable*. On his way home one night from the local store in a Los Angeles suburb, shy salesman Harry Balbo (Sean Patrick Flanery who also played in the movie *Powder*) witnesses female vampire, Tatiana played by Charlotte Ayannah, violently rip off her victim's head. When no one believes Harry's claims about a vampire, he sets out to trap the bloodthirsty killer. With the help of vampire hunter Strickland played by Michael Biehn, and using himself as bait, Harry imprisons the beautiful Tatiana in his basement, to stop her from killing ... falling in love with her in the process. Without a source of flesh blood, Tatiana faces certain death. Not wanting to kill such a remarkable creature, Harry is faced with an impossible choice - give in to her seductive charms or save lives instead of feeding her hunger.

Blood Ties

Blood Ties was a Canadian television series based on the *Blood Books* by author Tanya Huff. It premiered in the United States on *Lifetime Television* and was also bought by UK channel. In May 2008, Lifetime declined to renew the series, but the Canadian production company, Kaleidoscope Entertainment Inc., was still seeking production partners to bring the show back. This show features the character Vicki Nelson, a private investigator who specializes in solving supernatural crimes. Together with her assistant, Coreen; Vicki's ex-partner (and lover), Mike; and the sexy 450-year-old vampire, Henry, Vicki finds herself delving ever deeper into the secrets of the mystical world, all the while torn between her allegiance to Mike and her growing attraction to Henry. During an interview with the original books creator, Huff was asked what she thought of the vampire genre is so popular. She replied "There is certainly a lot of debate and discussion about it, and I have no idea. I think part of it is because we are all fascinated by the idea of immortality. And, from the very beginning, the vampire has always been tied to sex…. Kyle Schmid is just amazing. He's so good at showing he's 480 years old. He makes one hell of a sexy vampire too."

This proves problematic for Vickie, as she finds herself in a love triangle between the two men, which I suspect would truly be the case in real life.

True Blood

Vampires quickly becoming a hit on late night television is nothing new, since *Dark Shadows* and *Forever Knight*. Alan Ball's new HBO series *True Blood* based on the semi-popular books, by Charlaine Harris, where vampires and sexuality are pushed to the limit on this series and portrays vampires seeking "vampire rights" similar to the outcry politically for gay people as a mirror of the real world. These victims, like gays in the years past are beaten up by southern bigots (who would have thought that) who say things like "God hates fangs," and it certainly has the same ring to it as the phrase, "God hates Fags" slogan. It highlights the cultural struggle of acceptance and rejection of the vampires, showing clear parallels to gay rights throughout the show. Like Anne Rice, Alan Ball is an outspoken advocate for equal rights for homosexuals Ball, who enjoyed success with the funeral home family melodrama *Six Feet Under*, now with *True Blood* shows us a glimpse of sexual freedom and has made ambivalent comments about the way his vampires uncannily seem to resemble gay people. "For me, part of the fun of this whole series is that it's about vampires, so it's not that serious," he told the Los Angeles Times. "However, they do work as a metaphor for gays . . . for anyone that's misunderstood. At the same time it's not a metaphor at all."

Given the prevailing bigoted attitude I didn't think I'd care for it, but found myself drawn into a few of the shows, so I may watch them all. This erotic vampire drama set in the Bible belt Deep South, whose culture the show depicts primarily as a mixture of bigoted rednecks and Creole perverts, *True Blood*'s main human characters are nice white girl Sookie and her best friend, the sarcastic African American girl, Tara. Sookie's romantic involvement with Bill the vampire and Tara's outspoken comments about racism (as well as her gay cousin's porno webcam business clearly puts both race and sexual orientation as a primary underlying meaning to the whole vampire rights. Fiction is but a distorted mirror image to our real world – art imitates life, and especially of racial and sexual minorities, and becomes obvious here that the vampires are hated for their sexual identities far more than any kind of racial issues. The main plot arc of this season is set in motion when women who have sex with vampires start getting killed. Vampires also hang out in special vampire bars which again could be interpreted as symbolic of modern day gay bars. People who have sex with vampires are called "fang bangers," which again raises the question of its allusion to "gang bangers." But ultimately this slur is not about being ghetto but about sex - primary thing that seems to enrage humans about the vampires is their sexuality. It's certainly what drives them to violence against the vampires. Humans are already killing the women in Sookie's town who have sex with vamps, and they also bash the vamps who mess around with human women. In a recent episode, a group of angry rednecks succeeds in luring four vamps - two of whom had been having sex with humans - to being burned in coffins containing boiling blood. Two more drug addicts attempt to kill Bill by draining his blood so they could sell it on the black market as V-juice, a play on the drug ecstasy. This V-juice is renowned for its Viagra-like properties. The Japanese have concocted an artificial blood cocktail (a substitute for actual blood) called True Blood. This allows vampires to suddenly be able to "come out of the closet" so to speak, thus trying to fit in a society of the living.

Milly Williamson, author of *The Lure of the Vampire: Gender, Fiction* and *Fandom from Bram Stoker to Buffy the Vampire Slayer*, says changing cultural depictions of vampires reveals much about human society itself. "There has been a general shift", she says, from the vampire as exotic foreigner - as depicted in Romantic poetry in the 19th Century and most famously in Bram Stoker's 1897 novel *Dracula* - to the vampire as edgy "outsider...From the 1970s, the vampire has achieved a cool, bad boy, exotic and sexy image", she says. "And he has become a sympathetic creature, someone we feel for."

This is not entirely new, she points out. Right from the Romantic period in the 19th Century, when there was widespread fascination with Eastern European "vampyrs", the vampire has been a "pathos-filled creature who has been at odds with his ontology and his innate desires, and who has struggled with them", says Williamson. Yet it is significant, she says, that this aspect of vampire lore has risen to prominence since the 1970s. The vampire is a rich and very flexible symbol of so many different things", she says. "He can be a threat to us and our everyday lives - or he can be an enticement away from our everyday lives. "It is interesting that in the 1980s, in the era of Reagan and Thatcher, the vampire even became a kind of symbol of family values. The vampire films *The Lost Boys* and *Near Dark* (both released in 1987) are really about holding families together, whether it's the vampire family or the human family." Yet, she points out, even in those movies the vampires retained the post-1970s outsider appeal. In *The Lost Boys* the vampires are cool kids with peroxide blonde hair; in *Near Dark* they are cowboy types who flirt, drink and play pool on the outskirts of Oklahoma.

Vampires, once threatening, become alluring, tantalizing, especially during the social upheavals of the 1960s. "The counterculture changed the way we view those who are 'outside' of traditional society", she says. "It celebrated 'outsider status' rather than denigrating it." Authors like Anne Rice combined her views on outsiders, fact and fictional and gave us the clearest version of androgynous a look and style the Goth movement adopted vampire imagery because they *identified with the scapegoat aspect of the vampire, who is always outside of society*, says Bruce McClelland, self-proclaimed vampirologist and author of *Slayers and their Vampires: A History of the Killing the Dead.* To this counterculture, that ultimate outsider is the vampire, who stalks and feasts on the ordinary humans of mainstream society acceptable, even a champion they feel sympathetic towards. McClelland says, *"What changes is not so much the vampire, but rather our attitudes toward being outsiders, heretics."* In his extensive studies of the cult of the vampire, that the word Vampir emerged in Slavic societies around the 15th Century to describe those considered to be outside the Christian community. Vampires had even become a symbol of industrial society sapping people's will. As we'll see later, it expanded to a new subculture beyond the Goth, to Vampire lifestyle.

Pornography and the Vampire

Of all the things sexually arousing for most audiences, adult video is the most prolific. Taping into the vampire as a means to titillate bears scrutiny then, and more than an obvious, simplistic idea of cleavage and fangs equates arousal! In the nineteenth century, vampirism was a clinical phenomenon, which also included a series of relative 'horror movie' themes, such as necrophagia and necrophilia. While zombie movies and books have their own place of study, they are nonetheless connected as the original vampire is also undead, living off the host of a living human and can even be turned into the same creature as a zombie if certain conditions are met. *Varney the Vampire* mentioned sex as a dreamlike state in the recipient. Vampires elicit fear which builds the heartbeat, as does any form of arousal. Death is a transformation; the allure is beating death by living again. Poppy Z Brite once said, Vampires laugh in the face of safe sex, and he lives forever."

Dracula Sucks

The year 1979 saw the advent of one of the most famous vampire porn's ever filmed. This low budget porn film depicts Jamie Gillis, who surprisingly does an excellent portrayal of Dracula, giving superb homage to Bela Lugosi,

"Children of the night, what music they make". Richard Bulikas also has Renfield's insane laugh down superbly, "My cries at night, they might disturb Miss Mina." Even the fake flapping bat on a string is hilarious. Reggie Nalder plays an excellent Dr. Van Helsing, and the music score, largely classical, is well chosen. Periodically an intercom interjects with odd comments; "Dr. Silver report to room 22 for a lobotomy." Some incest was implied in scenes, as well as a necrophilia scene with Mike Ranger and the 'undead' Serena. These are all played tongue in cheek, and work well within the context of the film. Seka, a classic porn star had a brief, but luminous, appearance. John Holmes, whose acting is limited to his impressive endowment, had two scenes.

Les Vampyres

James Avalon's *Les Vampyres* from 2001, produced by Metro Cal Vista Video featured adult actress Syren. Unlike many triple X rated movies flooding the market, this one has more than decent acting, a full plot and absolutely gorgeous sets. A young couple in love arrive at a manor were they are joined by three exotic vampiresses. The sequel lacked the same quality in the writing, but I digress.

A slew of soft core porn films have been done, such as *Misty's Secret*, *Vampire's Seduction Double Feature*, *American Vampire in Paris* starring low budget actress Misty Mundae;

Tina Krause in 2005, also in *Lust for Dracula*, and others like *Vamps* and *Vamps 2: Blood Sisters* with Rob Calvert, *Countess Dracula's Orgy of Blood*. In *Lesbian Vampire* she wore a Catholic school girl and meekly attempted to ward off a lesbian vampiress, proclaiming, "Forgive me Father, for I'm about to be a very naughty girl."

In *Rise: Blood Hunter*, available in both R and Unrated versions, is Lucy Liu's debut as an undead femme fatale. In it, Liu plays the investigative reporter Sadie Blake, who writes for the L.A. Weekly. She is out for revenge shortly after she awakens to find herself in a morgue. As a freshly turned vampire, she tracks down the vampire cult that is taking over Los Angeles. Although this is not actually soft-core porn, this movie does show us a rather explicit lesbian scene. It features a not-so-average plot as it becomes a "vampire kills her killers" movie. It was well done and I consider it as good, if not better, than *Insatiable*.

Allure of the Vampire by Corvis Nocturnum

Allure of the Vampire by Corvis Nocturnum

The Master, copyright by Corvis Nocturnum

Chapter Three

The Vampire in Art

Behind the boathouse I'll show you my dark secret I'm not gonna lie I want you for mine. My blushing bride My lover, be my lover, yeah...~ Toadies, Possum Kingdom

A while back I recall a conversation with a dear friend where she mentioned to me about the song by Toadies called *Possum Kingdom* possibly being about vampires. With lyrics in it like "I can promise you ...you'll stay as beautiful... With dark hair... And soft skin...forever ....Forever", I tended to agree. After researching it years later, I found a few interesting things out. First, we weren't alone in that thought. And secondly, the band was cryptic in its answer as to the exact meaning. An interview back in 1995 by RIP Magazine revealed the nature of the song was like most of Toadies' tunes, are stories, as Umbarger explained, "They're just these silly stories he's (Lewis) heard his family tell. Like Tyler and *Possum Kingdom* are just like stories...In Texas, there's just this big storytelling thing - whenever your family gets together, they sit and talk and tell all these stories. *Possum Kingdom* is a ghost story."

"Possum Kingdom is a lake. One of the ten best fishin' spots in the U.S. ," Lewis commented.

When asked if it a about a ghost or vampire at the lake, everyone laughed and Lewis replied, "I don't know."

"It's not about vampires," Umbarger insists. "Even though we have a big underground vampire following in Florida. They come with their teeth and everything. I'm not lying about that, that's a real story. They'll show up and you'll be talking to someone, and they'll smile and it's like, 'Jesus Christ! You've got fangs!' And they're like, 'Yeah. It's a vampire thing.' So we have this big vampire underground following, and *Possum Kingdom* has kind of stirred it up." So what's it really about, then, he was asked.

Without hesitation, Lewis said, "Vampires."

What I find curious about the whole thing is what they believe a vampire to be like is projected into mere song lyrics solely from the consensus of popular opinion.

Some fans of vampires are influenced purely from what they see and hear, like a comment sent to me: *For me myself the allure is simply to see what the media comes up with. I am attracted to vampires because it is what I am, always has been and always will be. I do not find them appealing or erotic in themselves, but like everyone else if I were to meet someone I found that way, then I would. Vampires tend to be attracted to each other in a nonsexual way--we can sense each other sometimes, and that is a form of attraction though not erotic. If we find a certain person erotic he may or may not be vampire. More than likely he will be, for that is who understands us, another one of what we are, and understands where we have been in life, and what has happened along the way. Much like many people, like attracts like.*

What does the future hold for vampires and their fans beyond what we have already seen in books and other media? Only time will reveal what's in store. But now let's examine the results of no longer simply being observers in this and next chapter.

Performance Art

The sexualized vampire is not just expressed in art by way of paintings and computer graphics, but quite heavily in music. As mentioned in the segment on Lestat from Queen of the Damned, this 'vampire rock god' so to speak, is visually a perfect merger of both archetypes that has its place in real life, as much as it has in fiction. The sound track from the film as well as the movie itself featured vocals and music from prominent bands ranging from Marylyn Manson to Korn's Jonathan Davis. More than a few bands have used the vampire motif as their vehicle to get attention. One such band is Theatre des Vampires, whose releases from Plastic Head Records have certainly been successfully executed.

We can see why this might be the case when we examine their dark appearance combined with the somber lyrics that so pointedly define these Goth metal misfits. Looking at it objectively, neither the fans nor the stars feel they fit into society's norms, so gravitating toward the imagery expressed by these iconic figures should be expected.

Both are equally type cast in fiction and film as misunderstood loners and both vampires and rockers have exuded a sexual attraction in that bad boy way. Tall, thin and most often androgynous musicians clad in tight black leather pants and long trench coats on stage bear a strong resemblance to the angst ridden vampires of Anne Rice's books. A group calling itself Lestat blatantly carries this idea to the forefront. Unlike the bemoaning, whining Louis, Lestat by the second book is a performer and rule breaker, like the rockers Motley Crue, Guns N' Roses, and other similar bands in attitude and fame, etc. He takes on a Nietzschean attitude of Nihilism and contempt for the world he came from, and challenges the Elders, similar to the archetype Satan opposing 'righteousness'. The symbolic eternal outsider he is, Lestat sees a secular world raw and honest in its fury. Quite fitting for him, indeed.

Anders Manga

Fans with similar interests can relate, and both Goths and vampire lovers heavily into metal music thrive on the energy and sound at nightclubs and concerts. With an astounding four albums in three years Anders Manga has gone from unknown to being featured in Gothic Beauty magazine and headlining one Goth/Vampire ball or event after another. He has a lengthy background in the horror and fetish film world, with which he cleverly blends into his musical career that began less than two years ago. Anders, originally from Charlotte, North Carolina, took over the world of Electronica with determination, ability, and coupled with his fans on the Internet was launched him into fame. *One Up for the Dying* arrived in 2005 described by DJs as 'gothtronica'. His first single, *We Won't Stay Dead*, became an international hit, a fantastic blend of Gothic melodramatics in black and white video with a riveting pulsing sound of Goth industrial. Early in 2006, Anders conjured up another release *Left on an All-Time Low*, as well as the later in 2006 he released his third album, *Welcome to the Horror Show*. Early in February of 2007, Anders released *Blood Lush* and went on another tour across America.

Like most of Anders Manga's works, songs like *There Will Be Blood* and *The Only* are disturbing, yet hauntingly beautiful at the same time. His songs are very touching, ranging from dream like to macabre, yet all have a deeply resonating quality that stirs the listener. One must wonder what goes through the mind of such a composer when he pens lyrics such as *Why are we wasting all these beautiful years*, from *Beautiful*, or *Burn all the bridges.... goodbye to the innocence. Heart of Black*, his newest release has certainly not shown any signs of relenting in harmonic sounding, yet disturbing videos!

At Dawn they Sleep and *Sleeping in the Fire* both does an amazing job of keeping on the edge of sanity yet the rhythm of the background almost takes you outside of your own thoughts while watching the videos. Clearly *At Dawn they Sleep* is a BDSM heavy song, but seems to imply the overall nature of those more found of the darkness. It touches so many deep emotions. He has performed nearly every major event for the dark subculture one can think of - from Dracula's Ball to The Black Sun Festival, Black Oaks

Savannah and the Anne Rice's Vampire Lestat Ball on Halloween in New Orleans, LA. With his powerful lyrics and deep vocals, he mesmerizes crowds with his hypnotic gaze – not unlike the vampire stare!

Ambient gothic music from Nox Arcana has delighted thousands of fans, putting out a great many albums in the last five years. Artist Joseph Vargo, featured in *Embracing the Darkness; Understanding Dark Subcultures* has long held the following opinion as well, saying *" I think it's basically a matter of taste and the difference in people's threshold for fear. Fear causes varying levels of anxiety. Some people love to be scared while others dread and detest the same sensation. I think many Goths identify with certain dark archetypes, in particular the vampire persona, because it exudes sensuality, dark mystery and power".*

Theatres Des Vampires

Theatres Des Vampires were amongst the progenitors of a sound that would later come to be known as Vampiric Metal. Yes, there is now a class of music called Vampire! Their maniacal search for all things Vampiric has resulted in a Gothic and horrifying image that has inspired a near-religious following from their fans. Initially inspired strongly by symphonic black metal, *Theatres Des Vampires* has since evolved a sound all their own; a masterful blend of influences ranging from gothic to classical, electronic to opera.

Theatres Des Vampires have created a personal style of melancholia and crepuscular melodies. The sepulchral wedding of Sonya Scarlet and her male counterpart creates a vocal incarnation that is both catchy and powerful. The band has produced seven albums in ten years, always under the big English label Plastic Head, and has become more famous with each passing year in Europe, South America, and Russia. The concerts and festivals all over the world are a testimony to this success. Highlights include festivals such as *Vampyria III in London* (1999), *Gods of Metal in Italy* (2000), *Gothic Treffen in Lipsia* (2003 and 2006), *Gotham in London* (2004), and the *Metal Female Voices Festival* in Belgium in (2006). In 2003 they toured Europe extensively alongside Christian Death, and in the same year recorded an album with *Valor* from *Christian Death* and Ian Pyras of *Cradle of Filth* as special guests. *Theatres Des Vampires* has no trouble drawing a crowd to their shows. Their theatrics have grown increasingly elaborate over the years, including such attractions as fireworks that have on occasion caused a bit of conflict with local laws of the countries where they are playing. Once, in 2003, a bishop in Italy was brought in to bless and exorcise the site of a *Theatres Des Vampires* show. The event was covered by Italian newspapers. Their live shows full of theatrical, bloody, horrifying glory, yet are sensual and harmonic. *Pleasure and Pain*, released by *Theatres Des Vampires* was published November 18, 2005. Music critics and fans consider it to be the best album of their career. Special guests on this album include Bruno Kramm from Das Ich, Flegias from *Necrodeath*, Dhiloz from *Ancient*, and members from *Ensoph* and *Stormlord* October 2006 marked the release of their first live DVD, which featured footage from their *The Addiction* tour of the same year.

Now with the release of *Desire of Damnation* in March 2007, the band set a new standard of quality in their sound and their production. I caught up with the bands lead vocalist and was delighted to detail past and present highlights. Scarlet: says, "*Well, everything started more than 10 years ago with the release of the demo 'Nosferatu eine symphonie des grauen', The following year the debut emerged, entitled 'Vampyrìsme, nècrophilie, nècrosadisme, nècrophagie'. This project was born by an idea of our ex singer Alexander and our guitar player, Robert, following the purpose to connect vampirical themes taken from old novels and Ann Rice books with an horrorific atmosphere that rise to its best point after the introduction of our keyboard palyer: Fabian, who has proven a prolific writing partner. In 1999 we secured a deal with the UK's Blackend records for their Vampire Chronicles, giving us the access to the arteries of the international scene with our obscure sound. At the end of the same year I came in the band as backing vocals CD after CD we find our own sound that can be defined a horrorific gothic metal that ever grown up and changes without loosing our style and emotions. In the past two years our line up is changed, Alexander left the band in the middle of 2004 to begin a solo career and I remained the only singer of Theatres des Vampires. We realized two CD female fronted during these 3 years: Pleasure and pain and Desires of Damnation. This is our new beginning, our sound represents a new era of vampirism, modern, gothic and powerful at the same time.*

Vlad and Sky

Vlad and Sky, two vampires and entertainers from New York, have been featured on A&E and Unsolved Mysteries. Vlad was very obliging in his call to me and I was delighted to have his perspective on vampires and performance art of fire breathing and dance. When asked about the connection between fire and the sexuality of vampires, he explained:

Fire is an element to be respected, not tamed. The hypnotic element, the glow of the flame is a spiritual thing. We see it as a spiritual way, being vampires, mixing the two together. He went on to say, *When I go to an audience member with flame in one hand and theirs in the other, it is a direct transfer of energy, a connection. With swallowing fire for the crowd it has a blanket effect.* He also told me, *element of sensuality is in each lighting of a torch, it's a big turn on for us, and people watching.*

Photograph © Jeffrey Grossman-Fire Performance By Sky Claudette Soto Mainstage WebsterHall New Years 2008

Commenting on his partner, Sky, who dances while holding lit objects and fire touching on their crotches, he says women in particular find themselves gravitating to it. That they equate fire with orgasm. The audience shares in this hypnotic effect, while they build and expand on it as a performance art, vampires and normal people in the crowd gravitate to it. *We believe vampirism is a sacred ritual of existence...the public is Puritanical in is sexuality.* While he fully admits he himself does not speak for everyone in the vampire subculture, he hopes that both their method of entertainment and education help the people understand them better. *For some others, of course, I do, but you cannot please everyone*, he added.

Vampires walk among us

The love of vampires has caused a mass movement of a subculture within the Goth crowd. The Vampire, or Vampyre as some wish to be termed, is marked by an obsessive fascination with, and emulation of, contemporary vampire lore, which pertains to everything from fashion and music to the actual exchange of blood.

As with most subcultures, the participants have a particular style of dress and makeup which in this case combine Antiquity, Goth, Victorian and other similar styles featured in vampire horror films.

The campire community does not calaim a direct identity as Goths due to the myriads of various negative stereotypes portrayed in the media and, as a result, dislike being associated with the other group. Of the real (sanguinarian and psychic, aka non-lifestyler) vampire community do not claim a direct identity as such. We'll explore parts of this subculture in depth in the last chapter.

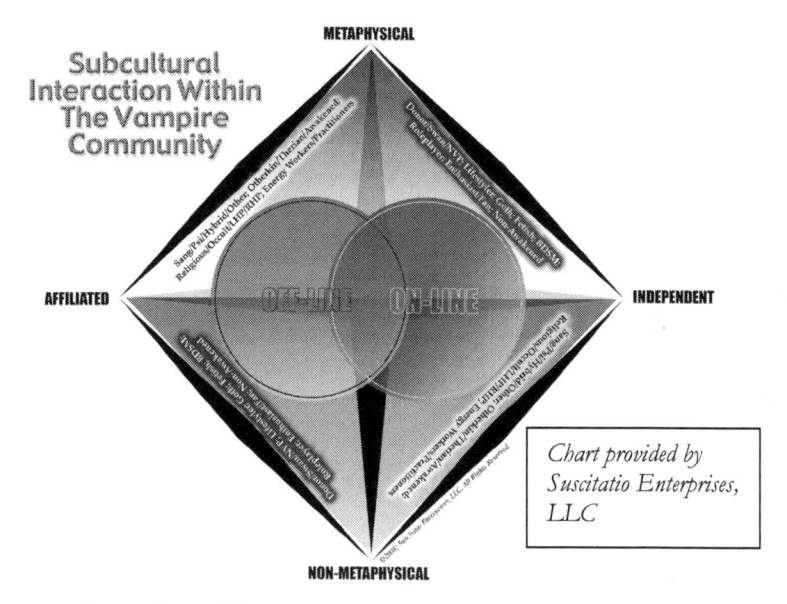

Subcultural Interaction Within The Vampire Community

Chart provided by Suscitatio Enterprises, LLC

Less than thirty percent are willing to claim Goth as part of their personal orientation, despite an undeniable connection and similar aesthetics, musical tastes, etc. A more organized aspect of the subculture are the members of Houses, very much like witches covens, but usually comprised of online and offline groups of varying size and structure. The most respected, established, and longest running Houses are those which are generally geographically focused around a specific region or those who adhere to a specific set of ideals comprised of an offline membership usually numbering fewer than twenty. Such Houses or Orders would include House Kheperu, House of the

Dreaming, House Sahjaza, House AVA (Atlanta Vampire Alliance), House Crimson Blade, House Quinotaur, House Dark Haven, House Lost Haven, Ordo Sekhemu, Ordo Strigoi Vii, and many others. A complete list of community resources are located in the appendix at the end of this book for those curious to venture online and seek more information.

The Sci-Fi Channel

In March 2004, the Sci-Fi Channel premiered a reality show called Mad Mad House. The program showcased a panel of alternative lifestylers whose job was to challenge a group of "straights" to rise above their normalcy and embrace open-minded spirituality and different ways of living. One of the so-called "alts" was real-life vampire Don Henrie. During the series he demonstrated his lifestyle, educated people on the truths of real vampirism, and demonstrated both psi and sanguine feeding techniques - on the air! His appearance drew as much excitement as it did controversy. He quickly became an icon within both the online and offline real vampire communities. Don has not only been a spokesperson in the media for the modern day vampire subculture but a living embodiment of the seductive archetype we have become accustomed to visualizing when discussing vampires.

Allure of the Vampire by Corvis Nocturnum

As Mad Mad House aired, and was re-aired for these past several years, The Vampire Don (as he was and is known) and his website (commonly known as TVD) attracted a rabidly devoted internet following- numbering 10,000 plus, again and again in its several reincarnations. His various other appearances in documentaries, panel shows, internet presentations, and print interviews drew even more and varied followers & fans. In Don's success, you can see different types and results of real Vampiric allure at work. After viewing his appearance on MMH, many vampires (active and latent) were drawn to his company. For many it was their first experience with another kindred spirit. They were enthralled! His allure also pulled the attention of thousands of vampire friends, vamp fans, and curiosity seekers. They came with great interest and many, many questions. Few left disappointed. On the fringes of his following were Don Henrie & MMH fans, vampire wannabees, troubled souls, delusionals & predators, fang groupies, and infatuated adolescent and teen girls (looking for a thrill or to upset off their parents). The one thing they shared was their seemingly uncontrollable reaction to Vampiric Allure- that certain intriguing draw to the elegantly dark & dangerous sensuality, For many, The Vampire Don Henrie represents the epitome of this allure. Insight provided by Lenore (aka: Mleep), TVD administrator from 2005 through 2008 and Founder of the online community forum, The Lost Children of the Oubliette. Dons' charisma and penetrating expression captivated audiences not only on that show but on several other television shows, such as A&E, The History Channel, and a National Geographic special as well as Maury Povich and an appearance on Tyra Bank's Halloween Special in 2008. Don has not only been a spokesperson in the media for modern day subculture but a living embodiment of the seductive vampire we have become accustomed to visualizing when mentioning vampires.

As the obsession with the vampire archetype drives some people to live a vampire lifestyle, we unfortunately see our share of extremists in action. However, fortunately certain key people lend their voices as experts, leaders and Elders in this subculture instilling ethics and proper behavior. We'll explore this facet in the last chapter.

The Vampire in Art

Vampirella

In 1964, Jim Warren, the publisher of *Famous Monsters of Filmland* and *Monster World*, decided to break into the comic book business with a quarterly Cleverly avoiding censors at the Comics Code Authority, Warren published *Creepy* in a magazine-sized format that wouldn't fit in the same racks as did most comic books. This allowed him to freely promote his works as a magazine for an adult audience. In 1969, he put out the most unforgettable vampiress in comic history, *Vampirella*. Vampirella's creator, Forrest J. Ackerman, was a collector of science fiction books and movie memorabilia.

Ackerman, known as "Forry" or "The Ackermonster" was influential in the formation, organization, and spread of science fiction fandom in its early years, and served as a key figure in the wider cultural perception of science fiction as a literary, art and film genre. Ackerman helped popularize the phrase *Sci-Fi*. Ackerman is remembered as the editor-writer of the magazine *Famous Monsters of Filmland*, as well as for being an occasional author, actor, and creator of *Vampirella*. Heavily laden with both horror and sex, this beauty's name was a nod to import *Barbarella*. This comic book vixen was clad in only her boots and a swimsuit, a fact that titillated young readers in all her forms from the oversized graphic novels to the current comic book and low budget live action film starring Talia Soto.

It originally was a thinly disguised soft core porn book, albeit with superb attention to painted cover and beautiful inked drawings inside. I owned one myself, but sadly lost it over the years. Clearly a marketing move, fantasy artist Frank Frazetta was commissioned to do the cover of the first issue and nearly every fantasy pinup artist for three decades has done a painting of Vampirella.

Roger Corman brought Warren's creation to the silver screen, and typical of private B movie companies, Corman adopted a volume-based ideology and commenced flooding the home video market, totally foregoing a national theatrical release.

Art of Tony Mauro

The art of Tony Mauro has been printed in books, generating thousands of fans worldwide, many of whom use his images on their computers as screensavers or backgrounds on MySpace and other social networking web sites.

His art is realistic and conveys the femme fatale as hauntingly beautiful and sexually suggestive. The final issue of the Gothic magazine *Dark Realms* showcased his work, a fitting place alongside the masterful vampire artist Joseph Vargo.

John Bolton

John Bolton is a major British artist based in the London area with a long history of erotic art, but certainly one of his greatest accomplishments has been the creation of the most dangerously erotic vampires ever.. Unfortunately, the Vampir portfolio has been long out of print. Publisher SQP produced a new series of Gallery Girls books in a brand new collection of bisexual vampire vixens, including the works of Diego Candia, Marco Baldi, Anibal Maraschi, Flores, Diego Florio, Perla Pilucki, Percy Ochoa, and Dario Hartmann.

Also, Frans Mensink through the Publisher NBM Eurotica produced *Kristina*, a Vampirella styled vampire with unquenchable lust for blood and sex! Awakening in the 21st century, she quickly commandeers multiple men as she hypnotizes victims. As we see in the sequel, after her resurrection from her last story, Kristina attempts to get back into the minds of her former slaves for a total sexual control.

Madame Webb Photography

I spoke to photographer Madame Webb about being deeply involved in the modern subculture of Vampyres.

Allure of the Vampire by Corvis Nocturnum

I asked if this shaped the direction of her art, and what inspired her. Madame Webb explained, *Yes, I am very involved in the Vampyre community at large and locally. I have never thought that it influenced my art but perhaps in a way it does. I adore opposite spectrum juxtaposition pieces, for instance featuring a model dressed in historic fashion in a modern setting, or capturing emotions. This could be my subconscious way of sharing my need for balance within my dayside and nightside life. To me personally, balance is the key to everything.*

© Madame Webb

Everything inspires me, from architecture, furniture, a piece of jewelry, the weather – I don't have specific sources. You can see from my photographic collections that I try to be as diverse as possible, just like I hope that I never develop 'a signature style' in my photographs because I want to be able to bend and move creatively within each project, every one of them being different. Every one of them bringing something new out in me, as well as the subject being photographed.

I asked her about her work, as she creates works of art and seems to place various figures together. This creates a rather poetic sense of life in a lifeless set, to which Webb says, *Beauty is everywhere – we just need to open our eyes. It's a view of how I like to view the world; dark, macabre, elegant, enchanting. I also feel that photographic subjects can be anything! Especially within the gothic subculture – gothic photographs don't all have to be about fashion and a live model with specific looks. There are so many other wonderful things we can capture on film, we shouldn't limit ourselves. And as a photographer, sometimes it is hard to find a model that can capture the particular idea or project that I am working on. Mannequins can fill that void.*

She also spoke of her own feelings on classical vampires of old and how they pertain to sexuality today; providing the following wisdom:

I personally feel that the very first vampire story, "The Vampyre" by John Palidori truly began our love affair with the vampire and influenced how most modern day stories and movies portray the vampire.

From how very forgein our every day mortal affairs seemed to them, our attraction to their death like demeanor, exuding charm and mystery which just sucks us, the victims, in and the vampire also pollutes the lives of others that they encounter.

In this day and age most people are looking for their own sense of individuality, and often people adopt an alternative self or character for them to live out their fantasies, perform better in their relationships and work atmosphere, and also for a sense of power which of course can delude the individual to having a sense of control over themselves and others. Some people take this 'character' too far becoming addicted to the power of control that they can achieve. There are many available resources available to become a 'predator type' personality, the internet, subculture events and clubs, fetishes, NLP (neuro-linguistic programming) hypnosis, books on psychology, mental and physical manipulation - all of which, if used negatively in abuse, could assist these predators in harming others around them.

The vampire is everything that most humans would dream to be. Sexy, strong, worldly, intelligent, powerful, wealthy, free of inhibitions, beyond the laws of society, and above all immortal.

I believe that a lot of women, because of circumstances in their lives, find comfort and familiarity in living in a 'victim' role. Helpless, looking for another to control their decisions, or just living to please another. Loosing or surrendering oneself to a vampire man, who can save you from death, illness, destruction, society, mundane every day actions.

For men, women are already surrounded in mystery and associated with blood, life and death, because of their menstruation cycle and childbearing abilities. For them the vampire woman is strong and confident, uses her sexual prowess for gains, her long sharp fangs pushing, penetrating through his skin making her the "symbolic phallic aggressor", changing the male female sexual roles around, becoming submissive to her every whim and demand. Or for a male vampire being able to penetrate its victim with their fangs and penis making them an ultimate symbol of power. Of course the "victim" type personality is not just limited to females, nor are the "submissive types" are only males, either sex can have these subconscious attributes.

Being a Living Vampyre myself, I have seen many dominant vampyre types take advantage of weak willed individuals around them. As well as many getting hurt emotionally, physically, loosing finances and businesses to others who prey on them.

Within the vampyre scene most leaders try and weed out people who we feel could or would take advantage of others, as well as we try to educate the naive beginners as to the dangers of what is out there for their own protection. We do our best to protect our kind, unfortunately we can not reach everyone.

Vampire Wear

Even some clothing companies, such as Vampire Wear have become involved in the sexuality of vampires, even in an amusing sort of way. I spoke with the founder of the company and asked her about the inspiration for Vampire Wear, especially the blood vial necklaces. Joanne explained, *The whole Vampire Wear idea came to me when I was in working in Australia. I seen shirts in a window at a shop that said "I survived a shark attack" they had holes in them like shark bites and fake blood on them. I thought shirts with vampire bites on the neck would be brilliant! I started designing the shirts with the bites embroidered on the neck and Vampire Wear was born.*

My husband Meko had this idea — "How would one become Immortal?" We have to come up with something that represents immortality. The answer of course was "Blood!" Inspired by the necklaces that funeral mortuaries have for ashes, I started making the necklaces with the vials that can be filled with blood, ashes, hair whatever strikes your fancy. The ones the mortuaries sell you can't see inside them and you also can't get them with bats, spiders, wolves and dragons. I offer the vials empty to fill yourself and also I have pre-filled ones with my own custom mix of fake blood and oil that looks exactly like real blood."

Her products were seen in an episode of the television show CSI: New York. I asked her about that show, and how she came to be involved in it. Joanne said, *"The CSI episode was excellent! I have received a lot of great feedback from people that seen the show. The prop master at CSI called and said they needed some vials. They got a mix of all the different vials I carry. He couldn't tell me what the episode was about exactly, the people that work on the show have to keep the story lines hush hush. When it aired it was exciting to see what they had done with them.* Her company has

Allure of the Vampire by Corvis Nocturnum

claim to fame from the cast of the movie *Blood Rayne* and others advertising their products. I asked her about meeting celebrity people in her line of work. *I supplied over 100 necklaces for the Blood Rayne movie premiere. They also gave out loads of the vampire bite tattoos I designed so that was really cool. It was shortly after the Blood Rayne premiere that I helped out as a consultant for an episode of Style Star featuring Angelina Jolie. I believe a lot of the great stuff that is happening for Vampire Wear.*

Vampire Wine

Vampires, women and wine combine, meeting with the company Vampire Wine. Rumor has it that the Vampire.com is actually owned by a circle of vampires and our company's founder, Michael Machat, an entertainment attorney from New York, is actually just a front. Whether he is commandeered by a vampire is still a subject for debate.

The first modern day Vampire Wine product introduced was a Syrah, of Algerian origin, that was bottled in France. In 1988, he sold the first five hundred bottles of this cuvee to Alice Cooper and MCA Records in

London, England, and began offering the wine in high-end London wine shops, including Selfridges. Owing to the nomadic nature of vampires in general, within a year of the Algerian release, the Vampire Board of Directors voted to move production to Verona, Italy – home of Romeo and Juliet.

At the beginning of the 1990's, Machat suddenly announced another change in production. This time, the vampires were going back to Transylvania. The early trips to Transylvania were treacherous to the psyche, and some who adventured with Michael came home with haunting dreams of the insanity they left behind. But by mid 1995, the blood of the vine began to stealthily trickle through New York and small pockets of America, becoming a prized possession for those in the know.

At the turn of the millennium, Faith Popcorn, the leading futurist and Nostradamus of marketing prophesized that Vampire Wine would spread and become a trend. Her prophecy came true. Soon thereafter, the blood of the vine appeared in *Maxim, Elle,* and *In Style* magazines, and was broadcast on *CNN Headline News, Food TV* and *MTV.*

Then unexpectedly, in September of 2006, the dark hitchhiker appeared again with new directions. The Vampire Wine should pack up and move once again – this time to Paso Robles, California – half-way between Los Angeles and

San Francisco. Not far from the Pacific Ocean, surrounded by hills full of intricate winding caves, this was a perfect hideout for vampires. Rural, but just 200 miles from two major metropolitan areas, it was also chosen because it is a perfect location in case the vampires get hungry. At Creston, where the wine is bottled, the mortal population is a mere 1,303 people.

So with scarce notice, Machat went out and recruited two well recognized nocturnal wine makers that have been creating and perfecting blends for centuries. Due to reasons pertaining to confidentiality, and for the immortal winemakers' own protection, the winemaker names cannot currently be revealed. Suffice it to say however, that the lead winemaker recently received a rating of 96 from the Wine Spectator – a grade almost unheard of. The new Vampire wines from Paso Robles express centuries of dedication by the immortals to wine making. So sip the "Blood of the Vine" as the company calls it and enjoy!

In the last century immortals had to adapt to the everlasting changes that led to the global village of today. As new indulgent products were developed and society's behavior changed, Vampires had to adjust to a new "fast-paced" reality. As a result Vampire vineyards now has expanded into other product lines such as vodka, energy drinks, cola and chocolate; all available to modern vampires at www.vampire.com.

Fangsmithing is the art of creating dental quality fangs that go over existing teeth. Father Sebastiaan, a Fangsmith and event promoter from the 1990's as well as in the United States, France, and elsewhere to this day explained his thoughts to me.

Fangsmithing is a unique business in this day of the internet, since it must be in person and thus more tangible and real. The fangsmith and the client often have to spend upwards of 30 minutes to an hour with each other per pair, the physical contract results in an energy exchange which has resulted in more awakenings than I can imagine. Since so many people in the vampyre subculture have gotten fangs as apart of their experience, thus each client became almost like an interview and I built a personal link with each one, each of us giving each other a little bit of each other.

As technology improves, the quality and amount of smiths continue to increase. About a hundred certified craftsmen are across the globe provide a variety of custom designed fang sets to their customers.

Cavrellero Fangs is a relatively new company and offers unique styles, as does Maven of *House Mavenlore*, Conan of *Laughing Skull Productions*, D'Nash of *Teeth By D'nash*, and Father Evan Christopher of the *Court of Lightning Bay*.

Other companies make contact lenses of various tints and unearthly hues, to make a complete transformation for the lifestyler, who may or may not select various older time period style clothing to walk the city streets or night clubs of major cities of the world.

Allure of the Vampire by Corvis Nocturnum

__Photo provided by Eva Morgan, model__

Chapter Four

Vampire Sexualis

―――――◆―――――

You see, it strikes me that this business of vampirism has strong connotations of sexual confusion. Bodily fluids being exchanged, that sort of thing. You have to ask where that comes from.
~ Dr. Edgar Vance, Blade Trinity

Sex, vampires and death are undeniably linked together. Although eroticism and death may be an odd combination, the sheer power of the vampire to defeat death holds a dark seduction all its own. Some people even fantasize about making love in a cemetery (I know a man who claims to have done so) are vampire and in general, Goths or just plain horror fans. Martin Riccardo wrote on this subject in *Liquid Dreams of Vampires* on how funeral parlors of the 1882 inspired the motif of French brothels. *One such room,* writes the author, *had a coffin, candles, incense, organ music, and walls covered with black satin…a lady of the evening in such a room would act the part of a lifeless corpse while the paying customer had his pleasure.* Although necrophilia is sometimes associated with such behavior, the death and sex connection is described as le petit morte, or little death. According to Riccardo, vampirism was used to describe this erotic attraction in France.

Until modern times it was also normal for a woman to give birth in her own bed. On both a real and symbolic level, the bedroom is charged with the emotions of the human condition....an individual might be born, make love, and die in the same room, possibly even in the same bed.

Dreams of both vampires and sex, especially with them is described in hundreds of cases in *Liquid Dreams*, and I highly recommend the work for more information. A special thanks to the author for his permission to quote him, here in the chapter incidentally. Michelle Belanger and I attended Gothic Fest in 2005 when her book *Psychic Vampire Codex* came out and I released *Embracing the Darkness*, and it was here I had the pleasure of meeting Mr. Riccardo. I'm pleased to say the Chicago native enjoyed my work and to this day we continue to converse on various subjects on 'vampirology' as experts call it While I don't profess to have a degree in psychology, I have studied it in college along with sociology and understand the profound impact the archetype of vampires have had on generations of mankind; leaving a deep-rooted passion in many of us.

Many view the strong erotic draw of the novel *Dracula* from a Freudian manner, discussing it as psychosexual Victorian fantasy; a violent image of the era's social and sexual taboos.

Psychology of the Vampire

According to Freud, behavior is "a product of one's personality which is personality is made up of three instincts, the id, which is driven by pleasure which calls for immediate gratification of its needs (sex and aggression) the ego, driven by reality and one's need for survival, and our superego, driven by moral perceptions that are influenced by societal expectations."

A vampire's wants can be categorized as the force that drives him; the goal of id as an oral pleasure, which was a taboo in Victorian times.

According to McNally and Florescu, "Sharing of blood is the deepest union of all, binding the lovers for eternity." Just before the Count forces Mina to drink his blood he says "And you, their best beloved one, are now to me, flesh of my flesh; blood of my blood; kin of my kin; my bountiful winepress for a while; and shall be later on my companion and my helper."

Freud acknowledges the struggle of female sexuality being suppressed and dominated by patriarchal society. As is the case of Ann Williams in *The Art of Darkness* where she says, "Better that a woman be a pure, dead virgin, better that she lose her head and her heart than to remain a seductive, 'voluptuous wanton' in this Victorian era". Such ideology is reinforced within a culture by the retelling of the myth.

According to what my sociology and psychology professor taught, such reinforcement helps create cultural myths and rituals by retelling stories that reinforce common values. This defines 'normal' versus deviant. A vampire's nature is in contrast to a society that insists upon a Judeo-Christian sense of moral order, especially the puritanical views on the so called 'proper roles' of our sexuality. Is it any wonder alternative subcultures live closer to the ideals of classical vampires than do the 'normal' people, who are visibly disturbed when shown what they secretly may desire? There is no denying the sexual element of modern Vampire literature. While the old fashioned Vampire was another form of plague carrying vermin, the new Vampire gave and received sexual pleasure. Freud studied the phenomena of sexual arousal through sado-masochistic action, as did the Marquis de Sade who wrote a couple of vampire romances, *Justine on les Malheurs de la Vertu* and *Juliette*.

Jung's version of an archetype

As mentioned earlier, we can see the sexual symbolism in the mythology of vampires from a psychoanalysts view; fangs and stakes as phallic. Yet, in Carl Jung's way of seeing personality development and motivational drive, he believed Freud's theory gave too much credit to human sexuality as the primary influence on personality and that it did not give leeway for the influence society and culture has on the development of personality.

While he maintained Freud's idea of conscious and unconscious mental processing, Jung believed there also to be a collective unconscious, a genetically inherited archive of all of humanity. Again, turning to my college texts, cultures share similar notions of morality, and they share similar symbols that can be translated across cultures with similar meaning. Within the collective unconscious are "archetypes, or primordial images, myths, and evolutionary symbols. A culture's oral-traditions and written-word are the means to continue the vampire myth and thus developing the archetype of the vampire.

Jung felt that archetypes were particularly important to personality and behavioral development because they "represent different potential ways in which we may express our humanness" that influence an individual's make up. The persona, which symbolizes the mask one wears to present a favorable impression of the self and to gain social acceptance; the shadow, which personifies the negative, antisocial, animalistic side of each person that must be tamed to avoid destructive behavior; anima, which depicts the unconscious feminine side of the male psyche; and the animus, which expresses the unconscious masculine side of the female psyche. .

According to Jung, emotional stability is gained only when the opposing archetypes in an individual are in balance. Archetypes, according to analytical theory, are influential in the development of personality and greatly influence both our emotions and behavior.

Myths that are intended to be "metaphors for how people act in real life." Archetypes are also seen as useful tools for diagnosing problems and understanding one's struggle and endurance. They are seen as symbols that help people overcome adversity, reveal prescriptions for change.

Access to one's inner problem solver, to one's courage to create change, to that 'inner hero' is an appealing quality found in the modern vampire. Rice's family of vampires drink from "the evil doer" according to Ramsland in *The Vampire Companion*. She describes the archetypal vampires as "… are larger-than-life, charismatic entities of power and mystery," at a 2006 meeting of the American Psychological Association. "They can defeat death, seduce anyone of their choosing, obliterate their enemies and stay up all night. What's not to like?"

As cultural icons, one must wonder if vampires developed Fruedian symbolic traits built upon centuries of folklore, or if they are part of a Jungian collective subconscious that we all have lurking in the back of our minds?

Perhaps it is a mixture of both.

Crimes and deviant behavior

Literally thousands of murders over the ages have been committed by those who believed they were vampires or who have been historically dubbed as such. Montague Summers once stated, "Cases of vampirism may be said to be in our time a rare occult phenomenon. Yet, whether we are justified in supposing that they are less frequent today than in past centuries I am far from certain. One thing is plain: not that they do not occur but that they are carefully hushed up and stifled."

Repression leads to two harmful forms of expressed behavior. One creates the unadjusted sexually stifled, the other extreme creates sexual deviants who lash out in horrific ways, from rape and torture to murder. Combined with the vampire mythos we see a pattern emerge over the ages.

Real night stalkers in history

In classical Gothic literature, vampires represented the repressed sexuality of straitlaced Victorian society; creatures of the night driven by beastly desires. Then as it is now, killers use the vampire archetype as their scapegoat.

Countess Bathory

Erzebet Bathory (also known as Elizabeth Bathory), was the first Hungarian female killer to be motivated The Blood Countess, as she became known, was the most infamous woman in history to inspire many vampires and various female killers.

She suffered from uncontrollable seizures and rages that became worse after she married a sadist who added to her cruel methods by which to discipline the servants. Many times she would beat them until they were near death.

Raymond T. McNally, in his book *Dracula Was A Woman*, suggests that Bram Stoker was influenced by tales of Bathory in the writing of Dracula, since the Count claimed to grow younger after bathing in the blood of the women had murdered. Bathory slapped a servant girl and her ring caught in the girl's skin. The Countess then rubbed the blood onto her own skin. Deluded into thinking it made her skin look younger, she began bathing in the blood of virgins, in an effort to retain her youth. The levels of cruelty and torturing of young women increased, as she would stick pins into various sensitive sections of her victims or beat them until their bones broke. During winter many women were taken outside, drenched in water, then abandoned, where they to froze to death. She did not get caught until she decided the blood of upper class women would suit her needs better.

The authorities decided to investigate after a murder in 1609 that Bathory tried to stage as a suicide. She was arrested the following year. During her trial a register was found in her home with the names of 650 victims. She was found guilty and imprisoned for life in a small room in her own tower where she died in 1614.

Women today still use her name as screen names or monikers for publicity, including a model appearing in *Blueblood* and *Bite Me!* online ezines and magazines.

Baron Gilles de Rais

During the 15th century a French aristocrat murdered hundreds of peasant children. After it was discovered the killer declared that torturing the innocent was "entirely for my own pleasure and physical delight, and for no other intention or end." Gilles sent servants out to gather children and bring them back to his castle. Why would a military hero and companion to Joan of Arc torture children? His excuse was that he was the hapless victim of his parent's amoral attitudes. Further, Gilles said evil took hold of him, "when I was left uncontrolled to do whatever I pleased and to take pleasure in illicit acts."

Bela Kiss

A family man and amateur astrologer, Hungarian Bela Kiss began his career as a serial murderer relatively late in life. In February 1912, at forty years of age, Kiss moved to the village of Czinkota with his wife Marie, some fifteen years his junior. Within just a matter of weeks, Marie had found herself a lover, Paul Bikari, and in December that year he sadly told his neighbors that the couple had run off together, leaving him alone. In place of his wife, Kiss hired an elderly housekeeper. She, in turn, learned to ignore the parade of women who came to spend time with the newly-eligible bachelor. In 1912 they both disappeared, with Kiss. Rumors and gossip abounded around the town, but no one ever linked the disappearance to him. When Kiss was drafted into the war in 1914, he never returned. Kiss had bought a number of metal drums, supposedly to store petrol. The army confiscated seven of them for supplies but after opening each one they found the preserved body of a naked female.

Autopsies indicated that they'd been strangled and had wounds on their neck, not to mention all were drained of blood. Over a dozen more barrels were discovered on the property, including a pair containing Kiss's wife and her lover. The police thought Kiss was dead, so they closed the cases. Later, in 1924, a deserter from the French Foreign Legion told officers about a fellow legionnaire who entertained the troops with tales of his proficiency with the garrote. The soldier's name was Hofman, and he matched descriptions of Bela Kiss, but the lead turned out to be a dead end. By the time Hungarian police were informed, the Legionnaire named "Hofman" had deserted, vanishing without a trace.

In 1932 New York homicide detective Henry Oswald was convinced that he had sighted Bela Kiss as he emerged from the Times Square subway station. Oswald was unshakable in his belief that Kiss, approaching seventy years of age, was living somewhere in New York. Unfortunately, the crowds of Times Square stopped Oswald from pursuing Kiss. In 1936, a rumor had been spread that Kiss was working as a janitor in apartments on Sixth Avenue. He managed to evade police, and there the trail grew cold. Whatever finally became of Bela Kiss, if he was ever in New York at all, remains a mystery. Bela Kiss was never caught and in Hungary he's remembered as 'the one who got away.'

Peter Kurten

The Monster of Dusseldorf was a necrophiliac, and rapist-murderer, by the name Peter Kurten. He learned to stab his victims to death while he was raping them, based in part on his claim that he got his start when a neighbor taught him how to torture animals. In 1913, in the locked room of an inn at Koln-Mulheim in the Rhine River Valley, on the second floor, a ten-year-old girl was found murdered in bed. It appeared that she had been disturbed while asleep and the investigators noticed bruises on her neck with two incisions on her throat. More bruises on the victim's genitals indicated penetration but no seminal fluid was there. While searching the crime scene, a handkerchief with Kurten's initials was found, which incidentally matched the girl's father, but he denied that it was his.

After serving sixteen years for an unrelated crime he returned to town, and again, a girl of eight or nine years old was discovered nude under a hedge. Two girls were murdered at a fair half a year later, with the five-year-old strangled and her throat slit, while the fourteen-year-old was strangled and beheaded.

Weeks later, a five-year-old disappeared and shortly Afterward a letter came to a local newspaper supposedly written by her killer offering a map to the body. Once found, it was discovered the child had been stabbed 36 times. Kurten confessed to everything, explaining he had committed numerous assaults, over a dozen murders, and admitted to drinking the blood from many of his victims because their blood excited him. Authorities say he told of how the blood arced over his head in a stream. This had excited him to orgasm, after which he consumed the blood.

Kurten detailed his forcible entry into young girls' room, where he first choked the girl, then slit her throat. Authorities say he told of how the blood flew over arc his head in a stream. This had excited him to orgasm, after which he consumed it. At the trial, defense psychiatrists had him declared him insane, but despite this the jury ignored them. Sentenced on nine counts of murder, he was executed in 1931. Kurten reportedly said he had "a desire to hear my own blood bubble forth" after the blade pierced him.

Psychopathia Sexualis

In 1886, a German neurologist named Dr. Richard von Krafft-Ebing studied compulsive and sexual aspects tied together in a multitude of vicious attacks. As I mentioned in the introduction, these criminals and early blood drinkers were cited in his work, *Psychopathia Sexualis*. Some 238 case histories were explored, delving into individual cases of violence if they contained a form of eroticism, all of which happened when blood was involved.

A documentary of Krafft-Ebing's work is available today and may be of interest to anyone studying serial killers.

People who like serial killers may find it interesting. Like rapists, these criminals are similar in the fact they enjoy the power over someone weaker than themselves. Adding in blood seems to be the factors combined that bring about intense eroticism. Granted this is much the same in viewers of vampire films, especially vampire porn, but the individuals described here took their fantasies to the most horrific extreme. Another man cut his arm for his wife to suck on because it aroused her.

"A great number of so-called lust murders depend upon combined sexual hyperesthesia and parasthesia. As a result of this perverse coloring of the feelings, further acts of bestiality with the corpse may result." Krafft-Ebing said, and states that it's generally accepted among experts on serial sex crimes that white males commit almost all of the recorded acts of a sexually deviant nature.

A few random killers that are lesser known for similar crimes as Kiss and Kurten:

France, in 1897, Joseph Vacher drank blood from the necks of a dozen murder victims

Argentina, fifteen women identified Florencio Roque Fernandez as the man who broke into their bedrooms and drank their blood.

Poland, Stanislav Modzieliewski was also identified by a woman he attacked, and he admitted that blood was delicious to him. In 1982, Juan Koltrun was dubbed "the Podlaski Vampire" after killing two of his seven rape victims and drinking their blood.

Rio de Janeiro, Marcello de Andrade, twenty-five, killed fourteen young boys in 1991, sodomizing them and drinking their blood as a means of becoming as beautiful as they were, the youngest victim was six years old.

Mexico, Magdalena Solis participated in a blood-drinking sex cult. She helped to convince villagers in Yerba Buena that she was a goddess and orchestrated blood rituals that involved numerous murders. When the human sacrifices were discovered outside the village, police came in and rounded up the cult.

Vampire killer, John Haigh, claimed that disturbing dreams created his unquenchable thirst for human blood, when he said, "I saw before me a forest of crucifixes, which gradually turned into trees. Suddenly the whole forest began to writhe and the trees, and to ooze blood. A man went to each tree catching the blood."

Modern Criminal Cases

The connection with such psychopathic disorders and murderous behavior is seen more recently in cases involving 'vampire cults'. Let's look at the most prominent ones.

Vampire Cults

Stephen Kent, a sociologist at the University of Alberta who studies cults, doesn't seem surprised about the bloody vampire tendencies of the adults and even teenagers involved killings. "It's highly plausible for a number of reasons," he says. "Some people can feel tremendous eroticism through drawing blood and pain and death." While people of all ages are seduced by cults, he says, teenagers are especially vulnerable because of loneliness, a need to belong, sexual confusion and family tensions.

The American Psychiatric Association and the United States Criminal Justice System work together in cases involving this form of mental illness, often labeled 'Sexual Deviance'. There have been a number of vampire-styled killings over the last thirty or so years. A few well-documented cases include the following:

1971 Wayne Boden was arrested for a series of murders that began in 1968. He handcuffed his victims, raped them, and then bit each one, sucking blood from their breasts.

1973 Kuno Hoffman in Hurnber, Germany, confessed to murdering two people and drinking their blood. He also dug up and drank the blood of several corpses. He was sentenced to life imprisonment.

1978 Andrei Chikatilo, the "Forest Strip Vampire," called himself a "mistake of nature," a "mad beast" after being arrested for the murders of over fifty people in the former

Soviet Union during the years of 1978 to 1990. He admitted to eating their body parts and drinking their blood.

1979 Richard Cottingham was arrested for raping, slashing, and drinking the blood of a young prostitute. It was later discovered that he had killed a number of women, and in most cases had bitten them and lapped up their blood.

1980 James P. Riva shot his grandmother and drank the blood coming from the wound. He later said that several years earlier he had begun to hear the voices of a vampire, who eventually had told him what to do and promised him eternal life for his actions.

1982 Julian Koltun of Warsaw, Poland, was sentenced to death for raping seven women and drinking their blood. Two of the women he killed.

1984 Renato Antonio Cirillo was tried for the rape and vampire-style biting of more than forty women.

1985 John Crutchley was arrested for raping a woman. He held her prisoner and drank much of her blood. It was later discovered that he had been drinking the blood of more willing donors for many years

1992 In Santa Cruz, California, Deborah Finch murdered Brandon McMichaels in what she called a suicide pact. She stabbed him twenty seven times and allegedly drank his blood.

1987 In San Francisco a student was jogging when he was forced into a van. The assailant slashed his cheek, drank his blood and then released him without further harm.

1998 Joshua Rudiger killed a woman and slashed three homeless men with a knife, telling authorities that "Prey is prey," believing himself to be a two-thousand year old vampire.

2002 Allan Menzie, convinced that Akasha from Queen of the Damned visited him him and offered immortality. He killed his friend by bludgeoning him and stabbing him forty-two times, after Thomas McKendrick insulted Akasha.

2002 Manuela and Daniel Ruda stabbed a friend sixty-six times and drank his blood. Role playing as vampires in Germany, they were arrested at a gas station with a chainsaw in their vehicle. Claiming to be ordered by Satan to commit crimes, they tried to excuse themselves of all responsibility.

2006 Nathaniel Chipps shots a fellow traveler in the head after an argument, and then steals a car. The twenty one year old killer explained his victim was a vampire whom he killed in self defense, although he admitted he was on drugs and hallucinating.

2006 Jasmine Richardson is the youngest person to be convicted in Canada of three counts of murder after slaying of her parents and younger brother. She and her twenty-three year old boyfriend, obsessed with Goths, vampires and monsters as the press called it.

2007 Tiffany Sutton ties up Robert McDaniel after they both used drugs and alcohol during sexual tryst. She sliced him and drank his blood. McDaniel struggled free and made it to a phone to call police.

Rod Ferrell

Even the mention of this case makes me recall a statement by Rice's infamous character Lestat, "*Evil is a point of view. God kills indiscriminately and so shall we. For no creatures under God are as we are, none so like him as ourselves.*" In 1987 one of the most publicized cases of vampire cults in our day hit the news. Seventeen-year-old Rod Ferrell pled guilty February 12, 1998 to killing a Florida couple with a crowbar. The leader of a teenage vampire cult, Ferrell was allegedly helped in the double slaying by his then-girlfriend, Charity Lynn Keesee, and two other members of the cult. In an attempt to gain sympathy and a lighter sentence, parents made it known his grandfather raped him when he was five years old. Rod also claimed that as a young child he was exposed to occult rituals and human sacrifices, was introduced to the *Dungeons & Dragons* role-playing game, and that his stepfather allegedly engaged in satanic rituals. As a young teen Rod walked in cemeteries at night, cut himself so others could drink his blood, and told people he was a 500-year-old vampire named "Vesago". He was engrossed in the role-playing game, Vampire: The Masquerade, and his mother allowed him to stay out all night, use drugs, and skip school.

  Heather Wendorf, allegedly told Rod that her parents were hurting her and she wanted him to come save her, but that he would have to kill them to do so. Ferrell and his friends arrived near the Wendorf home. He met Heather Wendorf down the road near her house. They entered through an unlocked door to the garage and searched the garage for weapons. Ferrell and Anderson then went inside the house, yanked one phone from the wall. Next they came across forty-nine-year-old Richard Wendorf, asleep on the couch. Ferrell beat him several times with the crowbar, fracturing his skull and giving him numerous chest wounds, including fractured ribs. As Richard Wendorf lay dying, Naoma Queen entered the kitchen, where she found Ferrell. Queen threw hot coffee on him and fought him, but Ferrell beat her down to the floor and struck her head with the crowbar. With Heather's parents dead, the two young men looted the house. They soon met up with the girls, and drove through Tallahassee and headed to New Orleans, presumably to meet famed vampire writer Anne Rice.

Ferrell's trial began on February 12, 1998. He pled guilty to the four charges against him. The jury was then given the task of determining if Ferrell should be given life in prison or death by Florida's electric chair.

Ferrell's lawyers argued that his young age should be a mitigating factor in his sentence, as well as his emotional age, which a psychiatrist placed at three years of age plus his extreme emotional and mental disturbance.

On February 23, the jury voted unanimously to give Ferrell the death sentence. Judge Jerry Lockett accepted the jury recommendation four days later and sentenced Ferrell to the electric chair. He was the youngest person in Florida to sit on death row at the time of his sentencing. Judge Lockett urged prosecutors to charge Heather Wendorf, pointing to unanswered questions about her parents' death and saying, "There is genuine evil in this world." Ferrell's mother, Sondra Gibson, said she felt her son did not deserve the death penalty, but endorsed the judge's suggestion about Wendorf. "There's one person walking around who's just as guilty as he is," she said.

Clinical Vampirism

Named after the mythical vampire, clinical vampirism is a rare, clinical entity characterized by periodic compulsive blood drinking coupled with an affinity to death. These cases documented in the medical literature only refer to those cases in which there is obvious psychosis. Little though is written about vampire subcultures. Patients usually have an irresistible urge for blood which is the ritual itself that mentally gives them relief. They are attracted to death and vampire mythos because they wish to experience it themselves. Clinical vampirism is one of the few pathological manifestations that blend both myth and reality with elements including schizophrenia, psychopathy (antisocial personality disorder) and perversity.

Medical Cases

It has been noted that clinical vampire's are individuals who most often get sexual satisfaction from drinking blood. Sometimes people suffering from "autovampirism" profess enjoyment in drinking their own blood, known as auto vampirism, a condition is not likely to be discovered except in cases due to random trips to the emergency room due to self-inflicted injuries. A case involving a woman four months pregnant was reported. The patient was repeatedly hospitalized for vomiting large amounts of blood but enjoyed the sight of it. Blood transfusions were ordered and the patient would unhook them, stating she would rather drink the blood. Initially the cause for the bleeding was unknown, but a through exam revealed several bleeding wounds at the base of her tongue. Apparently patient would suck and swallow her own blood. As with death of the "Vampiresis" mentioned earlier, an autopsy revealed the stomach contained blood.

Renfield's Syndrome

Psychiatrists are aware that there exists a behavior known as "clinical vampirism," which is a syndrome involving the delusion of actually being a vampire and feeling the need for blood. This is the mental patient in Stoker's *Dracula*, speculated to be based on Stoker himself, through a projection of his inferiority feelings due to the actor Washington Irving rejecting him. The Syndrome is the erotic attraction to blood and the idea that it conveys certain powers. In reality, this develops through fantasies involving sexual excitement.

The psychologist and author of *Bizarre Diseases of the Mind*, and *Vampires, Werewolves and Demons: twentieth century reports in the psychiatric literature*, Dr. Richard Noll, says that the clinical cases of vampirism ought to be called Renfield's Syndrome because they have a lot in common with the behavior of Renfield who eats insects in his cell because he craves their life force. This poor delusional fool thought he would become a vampire like his master. The psychologist explains:

The first stage is some event that happens before puberty where the child is excited in a sexual way by some event that involves blood injury or the ingestion of blood. At puberty it becomes fused with sexual fantasies, and the typical person with Renfield Syndrome begins with autovampirism. That is, they begin to drink their own blood and then move on to other living creatures. That's what we know from the few cases we have on record. It has fetishistic and compulsive components.

According to Noll, the condition starts with a key event in life, one that causes the experience of blood injury or the ingestion of blood to be exciting. After the onset of puberty, the excitement is experienced as sexual arousal. Throughout adolescence and adulthood, blood, both the presence of, and consumption of blood can also stimulate a sense of power and control. Noll has explained that Renfield's Syndrome usually begins with autovampirism and later progresses to the consumption of the blood of other creatures.

Renfield's Syndrome was also mentioned in an episode of CSI called *Committed*. It's important to note that Renfield's Syndrome also known as Clinical Vampirism is not recognized in the DSM-IV - Diagnostic and Statistical Manual of Mental Disorders. Due to a lack of throughout research, the media often portrays everyone associated with vampires and interest in blood as a criminal deviant.

Unfortunately, the real vampire community has to continually point out the distinct differences in their actions from that of the psychologically imbalanced as you'll see in the following passage by Merticus in an interview with *TAPS Paranormal Magazine* from October 2007:

"It's a fallacy at best to suggest that real vampires (psychic and/or sanguinarian) commit ritualistic crimes involving human sacrifice, cannibalism, and murder. Participants in the vampire community resent when the actions of mentally disturbed individuals are lauded as an example of an inextricable link to modern vampirism; some going further to insinuate that our subculture encourages and condones such behavior. Vampires don't engage in practices that harm donors and are bound by the laws governing their respective countries. Those who commit acts of violence or similarly egregious behavior within the vampire community are almost universally role players or dabblers who've lost touch with reality or long-term psychologically imbalanced persons who pose a threat to society whether acting under the guise of a "vampire" or engaging in normal life functions. Individuals such as Rod

Ferrell and Mathew Hardman were never members of the vampire community or by any stretch of the imagination what those in the community would consider "real vampires". Some in the media and individuals such as Dawn Perlmutter, Ph.D. in her 2003 paper The Forensics of Sacrifice: A Symbolic Analysis of Ritualistic Crime and book Investigating Religious Terrorism & Ritualistic Crimes, through poorly executed, unsubstantiated, and ethically questionable armchair "research", characterize vampires as criminals who engage in subversive and dangerous practices. Real vampires are mistakenly thrust into the same category of ritual animal or human sacrifice, fetishism, fanatical religious expression or cults, and labeled as unstable threats to themselves and others.

Vampires don't engage in moral indignation from any ostracism experienced as a result of vampirism nor are they hesitant to involve law enforcement when they witness violations of laws or endangerment to others. Several vampire organizations actually work with children and women abuse centers, teenage runaways, and with officials to recognize early warning signs and prevent criminal actions by wayward individuals. It's troubling to witness the pervasive negative attitude leveled against vampires when the actions of those unrelated by all accounts with the vampire community commit ritualistic crime linked only to vampirism by the involvement of "blood" or "blood consumption."

Others simply flaunt their erratic behavior with sex and bizarre mannerisms, absent of the drastic degrees of violence and criminal acts.

Marilyn Manson, ever pushing the limits of people's squeamish factor, says he is the vampire of love. While dating the nineteen-year-old actress Evan Rachel Wood, he says he preys on young women and wants to "consume" them.

Marilyn said in a magazine interview: "I've always thought that association, with the romanticism of vampires, was a bit too obvious a fit for me." But a vampire is only something that can be killed by stabbing it through the heart. And that's my weakness, metaphorically. Love can destroy you. But also a vampire is a character that only comes out…at night-time, and ultimately preys on young women. And drinks blood." He went on to say, "This idea of consuming someone, whether it's literal or a metaphor, is quite romantic." The controversial star also revealed he uses caviar as part of an extravagant sex game. "I can order caviar and throw it away. That's decadent, isn't it? I did it last night! The record company was paying though. And there was sex involved."

D. J. Williams, PhD stated the following brilliant observations in his article *Deviant Leisure: Rethinking The Good, the Bad, and the Ugly*, published in Leisure Sciences, Volume 31 - Issue 2 from March 2009:

Vampirism in psychiatric contexts may refer to rare psychoses or parasitic psychological attachments. The term vampire has been applied to some of the most extreme cases of violent crime including cannibalism, necrophilia and necrosadism. Given the common available discourses from which vampires are perceived, it is no wonder, then, that self-identified vampires remain underground for fear of being misunderstood....there seems to be some overlap between the vampire and BDSM worlds. Play that produces exposure to blood sometimes occurs in both worlds, although the meanings around these practices differ. Erotic power seems to be at the core of BDSM and much of vampirism....Like BDSM, vampire lifestyles seem to be creative, expressive forms of serious leisure that simply do not fit narrow social scripts."

Vampires and Fetish

Historical 'vampires' have influenced people in unusual ways, linking actions with erotic thoughts. Very closely linked between the depraved actions of aroused people and those who experience their sexuality through fetish may blur. Within all people lurk a darker side, and find release through pain. What separates them from the real monsters however, is the fine line of self control and intentions. A friend in the fetish/BDSM lifestyle, Lord Sedoh a self-professed happy sadist, recalls his feelings on vampires, saying "*I guess it's not necessarily the stories or mysticism of vampirism, but it's the real historic story of Vlad Dracula, The Impaler and how the metamorphosis of vampirism comes from the maniacal way in which he ruled and the use of terror in being the first European outpost against the Turks. In his unique way of putting death on display and making it both vividly gruesome and exquisitely torturous at first to the enemies of his empire abroad, and then to his enemies at home, he heightened the idea of blood-lust...next moving to the story of Lady Bathory and how her belief that the blood removed from young women being tortured for both the consumption of that blood and the bathing in the blood to keep her youth, also got my juices flowing and my imagination running wild for my own blood-lust. It is less about the fantasy aspect of vampires and more about the reality of the history that created the myths and legends."*

Blood fetishes

As mentioned in the previous section with *Psychopathia Sexualis*, blood fetishism is clinically called Hematolagnia and is used to describe the 'sexual interest for blood' within BDSM and vampire lifestyles.

These acts of using blood for sexual arousal are known as bloodsports or bloodplay and may involve the risk of spreading blood borne diseases. In most cases, such as in the BDSM community, the people doing so are in strictly controlled environments with medically trained practitioners involved in the scene. Knife play does not always have to result in drawing of blood. Suspension acts, which are done for ritual in some faiths and for meditative practices, violet wands, cutting, scarification, and needle play are also forms of BDSM which may either involve blood or heighten the energy from which vampires may feed if they are engaging in psychic vampirism.

Warwick Acott, age 39, from South Australian was found not guilty after being accused of assault and unlawful sex with a minor he met on a vampirefreaks.com. The girl said he stalked her for years with sexually offensive messages before pushing his way into her house on June 18, 2006 - when she was merely sixteen. According to her, her attacker first bite her breast, whipped her with a cat-o-nine tails, and then made her perform fellatio on him. His version was that the girl pursued him, telling him "he was gorgeous and she wanted to be his slave," after she discovered his profile on the site. He said he was flattered and fascinated when she told him she was a 'pain junkie'. During his trial, he told the jury he had no more contact with the girl after finding out she had lied about her age. Warwick claimed she tapped him on the shoulder in a sex shop, and asked him to buy her a whip for her sixteenth birthday. Further, he said she invited him home, and he admitted he whipped and bit her - at the girl's request. He denied that fellatio occurred, saying he pushed her away when she revealed sex would be unlawful due to her age. He admitted his verbal abuse, after she warned him she would "make him suffer." The girl admitted a series of lies in her evidence, including that Acott had cut her with a scalpel. Outside the court, Mr. Acott said he was relieved. "All I have to say is I'm very grateful to the jury, I'm pleased they came to the right verdict," he said.

Blood fetish and vampires as a lifestyle is revealed in great detail in Arlene Russo's book, *Vampire Nation* and I found it quite a good read.

A woman I came across in a Chicago club, known in the underground for fetish, named Lady Kitty, shared her feelings with me saying, *"They (vampires) are dark, forbidden, androgynous powerful, their bite promises either a sensual release into the arms of death or possibly a chance at eternal life with out the pain of sickness or old age. They are the ultimate predator, completely in control and the very top of the food chain. Power is sexy, in any form. Also many of them have the tortured soul, the love of mankind crossed with the need to feed... even those that embrace their predatory nature rarely do it with the clumsiness of most killers, they entrance and seduce, their prey comes willingly into their arms. I read Anne Rice's Vampire Chronicles my freshman year of high school, as I was becoming sexually active. They are very erotic books; her vampires are beyond gender which appealed to me. I loved the power exchange that took place between vampire and victim, so much more intense than the sex that was going on amongst my friends. The scenario of a vampire feeding (in books, movies and in my head) was not one of horror (I suppose I ignored the fact that most victims died) it was a willing surrender, an intimate opening of ones soul allowing their life (not just their blood but most vampires also get their memories, emotions, etc when feeding) to go into another. I began to experiment with that power exchange my self around the age of 18, and logically it led to drawing and then drinking blood from my partner (and allowing him to do the same to me) this took place during sex and on it's own, often mixed with some other bdsm activities. The experience of opening someone's flesh, the trust of allowing someone to open yours and the intoxicating power of drinking their blood (even in small amounts) is dizzying and wonderful and no other experience I have ever had compares. While I no longer drink the blood of my play partners (adult responsibilities make it to risky of a behavior sadly) I still draw blood on them(with needles or scalpels), and still bite them in a very vampiric way(without breaking the skin), taking energy instead of blood (not as tasty but still sexual) My husband is the only person I am currently fluid bonded with and he doesn't share my fascination so doesn't let me draw (and therefore taste) his blood but I hope to at some point have a stable lover with whom I can once again share this activity. It has been 14 years since I've tasted the blood of another and I still crave it. I know this sounds cheesy as hell but it's true. No I don't want to drink pints of the stuff; it makes you sick if you take to much... just a small amount, just a taste."*

I've found it common that teens raging with hormones are enamored by vampires, especially if they have a dark streak or are different in some way from others their age. They gravitate towards Rice, Hamilton, or even Meyer's works and often wish to identify with the vampire on some level.

Allure of the Vampire by Corvis Nocturnum

Allure of the Vampire by Corvis Nocturnum

Image courtesy Fractured Nightmare Photography, of model Jamie Mahon

Chapter Five

Vampires of our Day

"...vampires are very sensual, seductive and sexual beings. They have an atmosphere of allure to them that most others do not possess. When I feed I create a mingling of energies that can bring My donor and Myself to spiritual orgasm without sexual contact." ~ Lady Draconis

The good, the bad and the energy vamps

Television, since the reality show *Mad Mad House* featuring Don Henrie, has ever increasingly been showing the subculture of people who live as vampires. The vampire community is often loosely categorized by the three principal feeding methods. A blood vampire, or sanguinarian, is a living vampire who drinks blood out of some form of need. Blood may arouse them sexually, revitalize their physical, emotional, or spiritual well being, and even some believe it gives them extra strength.

Another type of vampiric feeding practice is psychic or psi vampirism. While some use "psi" and "psy" vampire interchangeably the most common spelling is inclusive of the "psi". It was explained by an online vampire as:

> *Psychic vampires, or psy-vamps, feed off of and manipulate energy and aura. Whether they take it from human beings, living organisms or even other psy-vamps, the effect on the victim is one of weakness and draining. The Vampire takes the energy into himself, thereby gaining vitality and strength. Many psy-vamps also use empath, an ablity to read a person's emotions and feelings with very little effort. Also, usually psy-vamps possess a skill almost like ESP, in that most can sense things with uncanny accuracy. In addition, there are also psi-vamps, which use energy in much the same way as psy-vamps, but can also feed off of other energy sources (electricity, storms, even sunlight).*
>
> *A social vampire of vampyre is also a living vampire who acts and dresses like a stereotypical "undead vampire". Some vampires of this category are more involved than others, drinking blood, getting their canines elongated and even sleeping in coffins. They do this if nothing else but to mimic an undead vampire's lifestyle. They may or may not possess the taint of vampirism, but have no special abilities or needs such as psy-vamps or blood vampires might.*

A hybrid vampire is understood to be able to feed from either blood or psychic methods as well as from other energetic-based sources Some, like a young woman named Sue said, they feel like outsiders that can relate, combining multiple felt needs – of blood, energy, and kinship "...*anyone who not only seeks the darkness for solace or to find oneself but also for those who like a little something different.*" It should be noted that a "social vampire" is most aptly termed "lifestyle vampire".

There are many misconceptions about the real vampire community and the symptoms experienced by those who identify as vampires. The following are some reflections on the problematic nature of defining vampirism from an interview for True-Ghost-Story.com on November 24, 2007 by Zero and Merticus of Suscitatio Enterprises, LLC: *Most of [the] misconceptions [with regards to vampires and vampirism] derive from the fact that the modern-day Vampire Community is using the word 'vampire' in a metaphorical sense, and from the tendency of outsiders to ignore the context of this use. When a member of this community describes themselves as a 'vampire,' they are not trying to tell you that they think they're a fictional character with supernatural powers, that they have trouble distinguishing between a role-playing game and reality, or that they hope you're gullible enough to believe that they're hundreds of years old and live in a castle. They're not even claiming* kinship with the folkloric monster that frightened the people of Central Europe, and has them performing vampire-banishing rituals to this day.

There is now a visible and vibrant community of people who are using the [vampire] label to describe themselves, but to this day there is no functioning definition of a real vampire. This is primarily because no one knows what the cause of the phenomenon actually is, and the community has coalesced around a set of loosely shared perceptions and symptoms rather than a central organizing principle. Therefore, we can describe some common experiences involved in being a vampire, but these shouldn't be taken as a definitive vampire checklist. There are no known necessary and sufficient conditions to be met before you can be a vampire. Likewise, there's no single definitive sign that someone is not a real vampire.

That said, the most common experience vampires share is the need to take in life energy or blood, from sources outside themselves, to maintain spiritual, psychic, and physical health. Blood-drinking, or sanguinarian, vampires have to consume small, polite amounts of human blood from willing donors... Feeding is absolutely a health necessity; [sanguinarian] vampires have reported many negative physical symptoms when trying to ignore this need to feed. Psychic vampires, or psivamps, feed on psychic energy. Some psivamps enter into relationships with donors in the same way that sanguinarian vampires do, while others consciously train themselves away from human energy altogether, either for convenience or as a result of personal ethics. Some psivamps report a natural affinity for feeding on natural sources such as elemental or *ambient natural energy. Others cultivate techniques for absorbing ambient energy from crowds and public places, so as not to take from any one source.*

Many vampires are nocturnal and have difficulty with school and day shift work. Many are visually photosensitive and get physically ill from sun exposure. Others will mention having unusual sensory perceptions, from the basic five senses, like light and smell sensitivity, to more esoteric extrasensory experiences. Many vampires reported seeing ghosts, having psychic dreams, or perceiving spirits, but some vampires have never had any ESP or PRE experiences. At this time, there is no scientific theory explaining why vampires need to feed, or why they tend to do so in very particular ways. It's at the center of the vampiric identity, intensely experienced, and yet to this day unexplainable. We hope that one day this need will be better understood and that our study [Vampirism & Energy Work Research Study] will serve as a catalyst for increasing scientific and medical interest in future research into this phenomenon.

Vampires, Blood and Sex Magic

The author would like to extend a thank you for the following article by Tau Peristera de Magdalene and Heosphoros Iacchus of Liberi Sanguinis Luciferi (www.solarphallic-cult.org):

In as much as the classical image of the vampire is one of life and death it is also one of blood and sex. While ethical psychic vampirism has become a more popular image in the modern vampire community, the folkloric origins of vampire stories feature ethereal or demonic creatures feeding on the life essence of a person, often until death. This "life essence" sometimes includes pranic energy, but it is more often in the form of blood or sexual fluid. In Western occultism, these images were perpetuated through the thinly veiled moralism of Victorian literature by occult practitioners such as Dion Fortune and Aleister Crowley. Blood and sex magick both center on an energetic exchange and therefore the idea of vampirism has always featured prominently in their practice. Since the Victorian period, vampires have been both reviled and embraced by occult practitioners. Regardless of the alternating views, ecstatic ritual and vampirism have always been intrinsically connected. The marriage between death, rebirth, and the sexual act is one that is repeated across many cultures and mythologies. La petite mort, a phrase used as a reference for the refractory period following sexual orgasm, is French for "the little death." Mors Justi, "death of the righteous," refers to death in union with orgasm and is the ultimate goal of Aleister Crowley's instructions on Eroto-comatose Lucidity in De Arte Magica. As we die in orgasm we are born in blood (semen). Likewise, as the victim of the folkloric vampire dies through the penetrating, blood-draining embrace she is reborn into everlasting life. Like vampirism, dark magick has been both revered and made into fodder for cheesy late night movies. The shadow side of the human conscious is drawn to these darker regions. We marvel at our own existence and fear our own mortality. These deep-seated emotions cause us to be fascinated with the archetypal images of death and immortality. The shadow self also tip-toes around the delicate issues of human morality, something by which the vampire archetype is not bound. The vampire of Victorian literature, for example, displays the mixed themes of pleasure, beauty, grotesqueness, decadence, decay, sex, death, cannibalistic blood lust, homosexuality, ritualism, sacrilege, and utter devotion.

Modern vampires define themselves in different ways but most fall somewhere between vampirism being a metaphysical condition requiring the constant replenishing of vital energies and life-stylers who wear the archetype as a fashion statement strictly for affect. Regardless of definition or presence of genuine pranic condition, they have chosen to identify with the word and the image 'vampire' for what it communicates. It delivers a message of mystery and desire, of sexuality and danger. The real "allure" of the modern vampire is that the characterization invokes those dark desires of the shadow self. Blood and sex magick also tap into the essence of the shadow self and achieve real contact with that inner knowledge of life and death.

On Magickal Paths and Vampirism

Much confusion has arisen with regard to the terms left and right hand. This is due mainly to the fact that most of us received our education in Eastern and Tantric ideas from the writings of the Victorian magickal revival of the late 19th and early 20th Century. Sexual mores of the day, combined with a post-enlightenment dualistic worldview, *caused many Westerners, particularly Madame Blavatsky, to project a quasi-Christian moralistic dichotomy upon the Eastern tantric terms vamacara and dakshinachara, rough translated left and right hand path, respectively.*

Later occultists, even Crowley, parroted, and elaborated on these trusted sources. This was in the same period that both glamorized and demonized the modern vampire archetype in fictional, religious, and medical literature.

The Left Hand Path, in its traditional meaning, addresses initiation through sexual rites and confrontation of social and personal taboos, or the shadow self. There is a strong sense of the feminine current - not in the sense of a good and kindly supreme goddess - but in the sense of true feminine nature (Shakti). The Left Hand Path is not inherently evil, as the Western definitions tend to state, but is considered so simply for its rebuke of social or tribal norms. This rebuke is intended to shake the personal consciousness loose from the grips of morality and allow it to ascend to godly awareness. The normal concepts of 'good' and 'evil' have no place in the left hand path - and in our opinion not in magick at all. There is an emphasis on THIS world and THIS place as the place and time for enlightenment rather than as some future or otherworldly reward; another point shared with the archetypal image of the vampire. Indulging in personal pleasures with the added benefit of shocking mainstream society does not qualify. Your personal taboos must be shaken as well.

Western sex magic begins with Eastern tantric traditions. (Do not make the mistake of thinking that "tantra" means sex or that it even needs to involve sex – it doesn't.) Traditional tantric practices do not always involve a partner, but when they do the energy exchange is cyclic. A circuit is formed between the practitioners and the energy is cycled until it has become something beyond the sum of the original invested energy. This, in theory – and if you posit that the vampric condition is one of natural energy deficiency - makes the traditional tantric exchange a less than optimal solution for vampric feeding because the initial investment is high on both sides. This is a two-way exchange.

There are however forms of tantric exchange that lend themselves to the vampiric condition. There are Left-Hand Path rites among Chinese Taoist dating back to early the Emperors in which feminine energy is absorbed by the male. This is achieved through multiple unions resulting in fierce feminine orgasms while withholding the male orgasm. There are also some extreme tantric sects that traffic with ethereal vampires such as the Dakini and the Vetala for sorcerous purposes. The cyclic feeding method of the caste system of House Khephru is an effective non-sexual but nonetheless tantric form of vampiric feeding. Western Sex Magick, while incorporating many elements of traditional Eastern tantra, is a very different thing altogether. The mechanics of these rituals are much more accommodating to the modern vampire's needs. The basic sex magick ritual involves an operator – in the case of feeding this would be the vampire – and a subject. Set and setting are established, whether this be a lengthy invocation or a simple seduction it doesn't really matter. The arousal of the subject is paramount. The operator should not be distracted by his or her own sexual desires – this *will mar the focus of the ritual. As the subject reaches orgasm that energy is harvested. In the case of non-vampiric ceremonial sex magick, this energy is directed toward the aim of the ritual – be it a devotion to a deity, the charging of a talisman, whatever. To adapt this for vampiric feeding, the operator (or vampire) would use the ritual to super-charge the energy and then at the pivotal moment feed on the energies. A psi-vamp would simply siphon off the energy as it occurred – most effectively from the muladara (or root charka) or the solar-plexus. DO NOT draw energy from the crown or heart charka unless you are really, absolutely, damn sure you know what you are doing and already have a good working energetic relationship with your subject. For sang vamps – a quick razor cut at the moment of orgasm will deliver a good supply of energy-imbued blood (RESEARCH BLOOD AND CUTTING SAFETY BEFORE TRYING THIS AT HOME!!). There is also the option of feeding on the mixture of charged sexual fluids and menstrual blood – us sex magicians don't buy into that Anne Rice "dead blood" bullshit. Alchemically, there is no more life-enriched blood than menstrual blood, with the possible exception of sexually charged menstrual blood. There is the final option of feeding solely on the sexual fluids – which alchemically speaking is identical to blood.*

Sex magick and the vampiric archetype go far beyond feeding though. Being "embraced by the vampire" is an allegory for facing death and finding some sort of heightened consciousness on the other side of mortal life. Facing the shadow self through psychic/initiatory death is that step beyond allegory but still shy of physical death. Ritual algolagnia (from Greek algos pain + lagneia lust) can be a powerful tool for self-transformation, self-realization, sensual-awaking, and personal liberation for self-proclaimed vampires and non-vampires alike.

(We do not use the terms Sado-Masochism or BDSM in this context because of the psychological and fetishistic connotations.)

Remember that the Left-Hand Path is about breaking taboos and pushing beyond boundaries – not just social but personal boundaries.

The mere fulfillment of personal kink fantasies is not enough to elevate the consciousness to spiritual and psychic liberation. There have to be some genuine buttons pushed in this process – some limits crossed, boundaries tested. The purpose of ritual algolagnia is a personal liberation through transformative shifts in the psyche – both conscious and unconscious. These transformative shifts are induced ritualistically using a mixture sexual excitation, mental and emotional duress, physical exhaustion, and pain as catalyses. It is one of the truest remaining forms of magickal initiation.

I spoke to a lady known as Mistress Dominae Drakonis; who appeared on the History Channel's MonsterQuest episode, *Vampires in America*. She spoke in length on her feelings on vampirism. (Note: Mistress Drakonis uses the 'My' as an identifier in the BDSM lifestyle as a self-descriptive form.)

She states, "Now as far as living vampires are concerned, well, I've read and studied all the material that is out there, and it's funny *because when I discovered that I had some 'traits' related to a psychic energy vampire, it really helped me understand what I had been dealing with for the longest time and why I was interacting with people the way I was. In fact, helping understand myself as a psychic vampire and the vampire persona itself in fiction, has frankly helped me understand a little bit more about myself and who I am as a person.*

With the emergence Twilight and the vampire craze a coming back, I am concerned that people will say they are vampires or pretend to be because it's the 'cool' thing to do. What they don't understand that the idea of 'vampirism' is a lot more than what they see in the movies. It's like for the longest time, when a vampire movie came out, mostly everyone took it as face value and said, ok, its a dark Gothy movie...something that can scare the hell out of people....something that perhaps someone wants to emulate...and that was that, no harm done. NOW, because you have the Gothic fetish and movements, more talk about subcultures good and bad as it relates to school violence and whatnot, and the increasing popularity of Paganism and Witchcraft, as well as acceptance in the mainstream, the vampire is getting a second look with the Twilight movie and series being used as a springboard and platform of conversation on talk shows and news programs. However, it's a shame that even with this exposure of the vampire, there are still some people who try to make a mockery of the whole thing. Those are the ones that never really lived as an outsider or with a dark heart at times....as I have.

What I was hoping to convey in My interview with Monsterquest was that I am a sane, rational, compassionate and loving woman who happens to also be a Vampire. So many times we are exploited because we are so different. But the truth is that other than our need to feed off of energy or blood, we lead fairly normal lives. I wanted others to know that my methods of blood feeding are safe, sanitary and most of all consensual. I do not feed off of anyone who is not agreeing to be fed upon. When it comes to blood feeding, My donors are lovers who have been tested for HIV and other transmitted diseases, as have I. And while blood feeding is very primal and powerful for me, it is something I treasure and hold sacred. It is a euphoric experience for both Myself and My donor - something that could not be compared to anything else.

I strive to educate others about True Vampirism and dispel the myths that surround us. I was hoping that the Monsterquest episode I agreed to do would help to educate others. Unfortunately, My interview was edited out and there was nothing truly meaningful left for the viewers to see."

I spent the week at the home of Don Henrie after he appeared on the *Tyra Banks' Halloween Special 2008*, where he made the best representation for the community out of all the guests on the panel. Don, like many others who appear in the public media, made it a point to mention that the thoughts expressed are his own.

In her online blog post Mistress Darkonis said: *"Tyra (on the vampire show fall of 2008) was an episode that they were considering me for. I was surprised by what the vampire guests chose to focus on during the show. It appeared that they looked down on 'humans' and in some cases on sexuality as well. They chose to highlight their special abilities of being strong, thinking of sexuality as something beneath them, being able to smell things better than others, being able to play with fire, etc. While I respect these guests it seems like they chose to emphasize their 'non-human' qualities..."*

It is obvious with this conflicting statement that individuals in the living vampire community do not agree on their views on sexuality, due to personal perspective and their own ideas of where individual social responsibility might begin. It should be noted that the vast majority of these people live in accordance to the law in regards to consensual sex as adults. It's important to realize that while speaking to a self-identified vampire or researching anything concerning modern vampirism, that most of the inhabitants of this subculture have their own variation to some degree or another in how they feel they embody the archetype and/or use or need *energy* in various forms.

When I asked her how she personally sees sexuality and vampirism in a classic sense and to the lifestyle, she said, *"Vampires have for the most part in modern media been portrayed as seductive, sexual predators. I am not an exception to that portrayal.*

While I do not 'hunt prey' I am quite powerful when I choose to feed. I am certainly very sexual as well. But there are many kinds of vampires and there are those who are not sexual. In My experience, vampires are very sensual, seductive and sexual beings. They have an atmosphere of allure to them that most others do not possess. When I feed I create a mingling of energies that can bring My donor and Myself to spiritual orgasm without sexual contact. However, engaging in physical sexual activity while feeding is a completely amazing experience. We are beautiful and seductive beings. Why deny the sexual aspect of ourselves?

We are beings full of empathy and the ability to connect deeper than most to our human donors. I don't feel that we should look down on humanity or deny that we are also human. We may have special qualities or abilities, but vampires who feel that they are not human are simply disillusioned.

I'd like to thank you for the opportunity to state My opinions. I'd also like to say that with vampires being such a great interest in the media it is important for True Vampires to help to educate others about who and what we truly are. Not to do so means that we are allowing the myths and misunderstandings to thrive and that in the long run can be quite devastating."

Tantric Sex and the Vampire

Before delving into the sexual predator section I'd take a moment to provide background on tantric sex practices, sensuality, and breath control, which is a significant part of sexuality for psychic or energy vampires. Sometimes participants in the BDSM and vampire community enjoy or even feel a strong need for the particular energy vibe that people give off during sex. I had a chance to participate in more than a few conversations by way of email in a forum called Tantric Vampires (http://tantricvampires.ning.com) where the founder of the group explained:

"The Vampire leaves a trail of satisfied and eager donors who willingly submit without prompt. While humans fail to use all of their senses, the Vampire works with all senses, and the most important sex organ, the brain. Seduction can be as simple as painting a vivid picture for our donors, something so satisfying to their psyche that they become more and more aroused with the thought of it. This can be created by delving into the deepest, darkest corners of their minds and finding that one fetish they have never shared with anyone and bringing it to the surface."

Unfortunately, there are emotional and sexual abusers enthralled by the concept of vampirism and those unfamiliar with being able to discern such individuals need to be cautious.

There are people who will use sex or simply their dominate personality to bend others to their will. In using another for their own sexual needs, they are dependant on their victims as much as they subtly force and manipulate those they chose to call on to be companions. By using sex as a tool they seduce and deeply entice people. Further, some of these victimizers will promise anything and everything to those they snare, lie, pretend to be their friend or lover, all the while draining the hapless newcomer to next to nothing. It is said absolute power corrupts absolutely, and unfortunately the allure of the vampire is a method for sociopaths cunning enough to slowly drain the life from someone, quite literally as Deacon Frost did in Blade; "Like human cattle....these people are our food." Some manipulate and abuse more than just the 'humans', preying on their own; no better than a person at a club slipping someone roofies. Even some go as far as becoming the center of attention to the entire community, drawing hundreds to them like the pied piper of Hamlin, mesmerizing and tapping into the need for love and connection. By using the lure and mystique of power offered to them they use sex and sometimes drugs to heighten the dependency of being associated with them. The vampire quickly becomes aware of the drives and needs of their victim, making it easy for the vampire to control them.

The vampire may provide sex, talents in any manner of way, and even force their victim to leave behind all else but the 'master.' Should the hapless victim start to realize what is going on the vampire may attempt to reestablish the romantic ties to reel them back in until control is regained. Such form of manipulation is also the pattern of spousal abusers, kidnappers, and even psychopaths.

A fragile state makes it even easier to hold a tight grip because unfortunately, not all people draw to the lifestyle of living this way. The mythic mind control or mesmerism in vampire folklore and film becomes real, a socio-psychic form of vampirism. Once the victim has been used to obtain the hidden goals or a better looking or more skilled alternative comes along, the relationship ends with the victim feeling isolated and frightened. They feel drained, in much the same way as blood loss, when in actuality they are unable or unwilling to see the truth behind the *failed* relationship. The lack of social skills, confidence, feelings of nihilism, and loner types create both the victim and the victimizer. This type of situation is not terribly common but some exist and it is the duty of the leaders or Elders of the vampire community to maintain self-control, education and serve as role models to show that the thrill of the hunt should remain in the volumes of fiction.

Many individuals in the vampire subculture have no psychiatric history, but are simply seeking relationships with other people and want to belong. Any sexual misconduct typically arises from an attention seeking behavior and is usually a quite rare and isolated incident. Fans looking for others to connect with have easy access to many others via the internet. There are hundreds of web sites where those who are curious about vampirism can go to gain information and network with others, a good deal of them I list in the back of this book. Many of these Web sites offer live chat rooms and bulletin boards where messages may be exchanged. Several magazines focus on the paranormal and horror, like *Fangoria* and *Rue Morgue,* and include articles on vampires and vampirism. Additionally, *Bite Me!* and my own creation, *The Ninth Gate* magazine, are also still in print.

Blue Blood is now only a web creation, but it used to be in print. Sadly, both *Carpe Noctem* and as I mentioned before, *Dark Realms* have ceased production. The internet seems to have been the death of printed magazines. Individuals and groups who try to educate and promote vampirism publish books, websites, and ezines on the subject. *Grave Yard Press* and *Dark Gothic Resurrected* magazines are both good. Teens and preteens today are modeling themselves after pop-media stars who play vampire roles, joining sites such as VampireFreaks.com (over one million accounts strong) and VampireRave.com. Neither VampireFreaks nor VampireRave are truly representative of the real vampire community as they are mainly just vampire fan and dark underground culture sites.

If you're looking to learn more about the real vampire community I'd recommend Joe Laycock's book *Vampires Today: The Truth About Modern Vampirism* and Michelle Belanger's anthology of various vampire perspectives titled *Vampires In Their Own Words*.

Both of these works are very valuable insights into the modern vampire community.

Vampires may influence the cross-over of fetish communities but the two are not always directly related. People in both communities are of mixed emotions on the subject of vampirism and may have nothing to do with each other. However, some do and even mix various lifestyles and even religions with the vampire archetype, such as with Temple of the Vampire.

A colleague of mine wrote an article I'd like to share.

Vampyric attraction and LaVey's Law of the Forbidden
By Miss Jenny, Co Founder of The Black Circle Productions.

There is but one common element of the archetype of the Vampyre that makes Nightkynde and Normal Folk alike feel the pull. It is The Law of the Forbidden. This principle is succinctly described in The Satanic Bible as the allure of the taboo or any kind of a delicious anomaly. Those of us of The Nightkynde obviously thrive on the extraordinary; we live and breathe it! And the Muggle Folk feel varying degrees of attraction for things unusual; as do most simple creatures for shiny things.

The Law of the Forbidden makes the Vampyre so appealing for various reasons. The simplest being the way he/she looks. Society (and my parents) would dictate that I'm not supposed to fall for a guy who looks like a Vampyre, but rather the 'Graham Wellington' type instead. Or at least one of the Bro-back Mountain bunch. And their sons are supposed to court Jessica Simpson, not Miss Jenny. And Gods forbid any Milquetoast offspring desire the same sex or multiple lovers; especially at once!

But as for us, we're attracted to Louis de Lioncourt, not Brad Pitt in broad daylight. And we'd take Vampyra over all three of Hef's latest strumpets any day. But for the Normal Folk, we; as well as the

Vampyre; are quite the exotic delicacy. Yet the *Vampyre* offers something else for each and every one of us: the gift of *Surrender*. For the Daytime Folk, the fantasy of a *Vampyre* seductor can fulfill sexual desires without any guilt because the *Vampyre* "takes" his/her victims. And to be on the receiving end of such an exchange, you are just that; a victim.

How luxurious to be liberated of such a burden! Be it sexual oppression sown by religion, patriarch-ism, homophobia or society in general - it's all out the window. Another example of this liberation includes a growingly typical male fantasy. As a professional Domme and a great lover of men in my personal life; I hear this one a lot; the concept of forced-bi situations. And it always starts off the same and I've heard it a million times:

"I lose a bet with my buddies and I get forced to..." you fill in the blank.

So I'll sic a Dom on him and he can enjoy the homoerotic debauchery without going to Hell. Or worse; being labeled a fag - it's the perfect crime!

This concept of passive sexuality can be traced back to Victorian times. And this is the era that brought us Bram Stoker's *Dracula, Varney the Vampire* and *Carmilla*. Very fitting, but also a time of extreme social and sexual oppression. And as we know; 'tis the perfect red velvet curtain for a thriving underground scene! In an aesthetically succulent time of gas-lit cobblestone streets, sconces, dusters worn with top hats and strict corsets; upstanding citizens savored these

Penny-Dreadfuls behind closed doors. To the green-fanged Fledgling; Penny-Dreadful novels were roughly the equivalent of Victorian porn.

In these forbidden tomes, the pages are graced with beautiful illustrations of slumbering Lovelies abed in their underthings with a handsome Fiend about to take her. Such a forbidden, decadent depiction would make even the most seasoned Libertine attain an erection! No doubt many a gentleman would live vicariously through this dashing Vampyric intruder. And how many of us ladies (and fops) have lounged' pon the Fainting Couch on a lonely evening in our dainties secretly hoping for such an Incubus? Perhaps there's more to the tales of Sleeping Beauty and Snow White than Herr Disney would have you believe...

One can see the same wonderfully naughty concept depicted in 1950's Pulp-Fiction paperbacks, horror movies, stag films and pin-up magazines; such as Beauty Parade, Eye-full and Titter. Here, a gal can be taken by anyone from a hood or a masher to the Creature of the Black Lagoon. Or even by circumstance; a Coppertone puppy, a faulty garter or a mere gust of wind. Even in seemingly innocent Looney Tunes and cartoons by Tex Avery and the fine fellas who brought us Tom and Jerry; the whole "Eeek! A mouse!!" bit is a classic example of something happening that shouldn't be happening.

Even for Nightkynde the Vampyre provides sweet Surrender. Firstly, he gives us an escape from the mundane, modern vanilla world. How delightful to have a lover that one doesn't have to explain the simplest Dark ideas to! No High Goth wants a DIY project on every date! Miss Jenny's ideal Gentleman Companion for the evening requires no lengthy dissertation of whom Oscar Wilde or Dani Filth is. And he would be well aware of the fact that Queen of the Damned was originally a glorious novel and naught a misleading, awful movie. He would also be of dapper attire and successfully manage to be aristocratically well-bred and a delightful rogue at the same time. And I would certainly hope that such a Gentleman of the Night would prefer the company of Ladies such as myself and my Dark Sisters than that of a typical 2010 Tiffany-Tuesday. (Please forgive the alliteration.)

Another manner in which the Vampyre provides Surrender to us is in the form of sexual relinquishment. 'Tis similar of the Surrender bestowed upon the Normal Folk, but the release has nothing to do with sexual guilt nor inhibitions. For Libertines of the Night...or Day; especially those of us with Type A (not the blood-type, mind you) personalities and lifestyles; Surrender is just what the doctor ordered..

Whether you are a teacher, an exotic dancer, a CEO, a performer or a Dom/me; what a treat it is to let someone else take hold of the reins. Business decisions, stage and seduction are fucking hard work! And BDSM sessions are hard-core choreography indeed. Everybody needs a break now and then. And a beguiling Vampyric male having his way with me would easily rival a Soccer Mom's afternoon at a day-spa. I'd like to be the Prey instead of the Predatoress for a change!

Even as a Dominant, the idea of ending a workday or an evening of performing on a relaxing pleasurable note would be quite the luxury. I would adore to unwind after a day of sessions with submissive clients. Who are, bless them; significantly older and balding and heavy-set. Or even after a date with a beautiful lad, with whom this Vampyric Mrs. Robinson must gently orchestrate everything; to return home and have my Jerome or Anthony, Sir Mensi, Draconis or Sieshan (or all five at once) ravish ME... T'would be sheer Valhalla... Ah, the Vampyre is truly a Luciferian hero for all he/she does for us. The Vampyre absolves us of shame, repression, responsibility and initiative. She sates us. He does all the work and gives us what we all need; literally and figuratively. And for that, all of us Creatures of both Vice and Virtue should be Infernally grateful.

Vampire Ethics

Ethics are a crucial part of the real vampire community and are generally followed or uphold in some form or fashion. Parallel to "normal everyday life" there is another side. We find that vampires exist in the dark nightclubs as well

Onyx, photo courtesy of model.

as are even soccer moms much the same as we occasionally find Satanists performing rituals who aren't necessarily Devil worshippers. In dealing with our fellow travelers in the dark, it is a razor's edge we walk. In a world rich in its mix of diverse and wondrous people, and each has their own story. Strangers stare in childlike awe or even whisper, but if you become accepted among any of them, treat them as you wish to be treated and above all be respectful.

This goes for anyone, at any stage of acceptance, which is sometimes forgotten. Ironically, respect and proper behavior which may be inconstant in the everyday lives of "regular" people, is often demanded, or rather expected, among the majority of people in so called "alternative" religions, lifestyles, and cultures.

No matter the title you hold or those in your presence bear in mind the old adage of attracting more bee's with honey. In nearly every subcultural community, Elders have laid out detailed documents of proper behavior, no matter how diverse the type. As much as it may shock the lay person, Satanists follow much more than a one might think; *The Eleven Rules of the Earth* and *The Nine Satanic Statements* for example. The vampire community has *The Black Veil* and other ethical documents.

Many of these written guidelines have their origins in Renaissance times where courtly behavior was expected. The medieval courtier of literature was a gentleman with a compilation of traits ranging from classical scholar, well dressed in their choice of attire, and a cut above the common man in public speaking. Just because vampires (Vampyres) may look or act different than the status quo, it doesn't preclude them from societal manners.

In fact, possessing the commonly shared intellect and individuality that made them outcasts is a hallmark of our predecessors. The writers of classics such as Byron, Poe, Shelly, and Stoker are such an influence on vampire and Goths Edwardian style of jewelry and dress. They even have a far reaching effect in many ways, to works of art by individuals such as Joseph Vargo, Brom, and even myself.

Etiquette in dark subcultures today originated from a bygone era where it was expected for one to act as a polished and refined as one could - exemplary specimens of human dignity and a living example of an ideal society. Those who ignore respect cause people in the community concern, however, the majority are good people who understand that the sexy attitude is just one component. A friend named Adam commented to me before we left to see the *Underworld: Rise of the Lycans*: when he said *"There are many things that make vampires sexy. From the way they move, to the way they feed. The act of feeding can be a major turn on. To the vampire, and to the donor. Whether the vampire drinks the person's blood, or absorbs the life energy itself. That is why most vampires live in cities. There are clods of this excess life energy. Not to say that is all they do far from it. For the most part they are like most people. Trying to live their lives the best they can.*

The only bad part is there are some who call them selves vampires, and can't tell fantasy from real life. Those are the people that cause all the trouble, and the good ones get the backlash!"

It's important to understand the attitude of the past in comparison of today, especially in dealing with issues among alternative people. There are areas of debate in ethics and safety among vampires. The giving and taking of blood is a touchy subject. Some cling to its necessity, whether it is symbolic, magickal, or for some physical necessity. The feeding type debate is common for many reasons. The primary two examples are for the purpose of psychology and of safety.

In an interview for ABCNews.com, Merticus, an elder and current administrator of the leadership network Voices of the Vampire Community, said that *his primary feeding method is pranic and tantric-sexual, meaning that he feeds on sexual energy and arousal. Although the precise reason for craving blood is unclear, "vampires cannot adequately sustain their own physical, mental or spiritual well-being without the taking of blood or vital life force energy from other sources, often human, Sanguine vampires feed by drinking human or animal blood but vary in their experience of blood-hunger",* he said. *They typically consume an ounce or less of blood at a time, usually no more than once a week. When blood is from human sources,* he said, *"It is consensual and facilitated through verbal or written contracts between vampires and donors. The vampire donor relationship is one of mutual respect and gratification,"* he adds, *"We make every effort to educate ourselves on safe feeding methods, basic anatomy and physiology, first aid, sterilization, disease prevention, and safer sex practices."*

While researching the concept of ethics among vampires, one community leader conveyed to me the following: *"The vampire community values community, respect, integrity, awareness, and safety. The community is comprised of individuals with diverse social backgrounds and spiritual paths. Although we may not agree with everyone's belief, practice, or tradition, we all have a common right to exist, and to participate in the community. The vampire community is the result of its members engaging in self-discovery; it is not a prefabricated identity. Whether one is a vampire or donor, a friend or supporter, the substance of the community is formed through our self-awareness and interaction. We are true to ourselves, and encourage self-awareness in others, so that we all can live according to our own aesthetics and consciences."*

There are several safety guidelines written by knowledgeable members of the vampire community and everyone should take heed of them. The protocol outlined in these documents will hopefully educate individuals to the dangers of blood borne diseases and improper blood letting techniques or energetic feeding practices. If for no other reason than following proper protocol, individuals new to the community will hopefully save themselves from AIDS and other STDs. Rules can be useful, even as a psychological tool.

If new members to the community want to attempt to "social climb", they need follow guidelines to save face and earn the respect of others. Many leaders make it mandatory that their members are checked for diseases. Since some aspects of BDSM involve blood play and because the erotic nature of vampires often overlaps, safer sex practices are encouraged.

Dangers do exist, especially online, where anyone can claim to be what ever they wish, egos rise to ridiculous levels. This sad fact rears its ugly head as witnessed in the news of true deviants who use the net as a stalking tool to find victims, as these serial killers pretending to be a good Master or Dominate seeking a Slave or Submissive. Alarming rates of people think they have to ignore common sense to be a subject under or with BDSM lifestylers. The law automatically assumes practitioners are deviants en masse, and sweep in, hence the secrecy generally found among any of these subcultures. Safe houses and guidelines have fortunately been appearing more and more.

On shows such as CSI the demeanor presented of most vampires is more than slightly skewed. A negative portrayal for entertainment, depicting vampires as deranged sociopaths instead of rational people who have a differing sense of style, needs, and beliefs. Television or movies portray the two extremes of good and bad in these kinds of groups. Granted, the images in fiction most of us see or read about are vile or anti-heroes like Lestat of the Anne Rice novels, or Laurel K. Hamilton's Jean-Claude. Likewise, they personify the 14th century dress, elegance and meticulously delivered speech. Like that of the homicide detective from Atlanta, GA, named Stephen O'Mallie. A bodyguard for vampire researcher Katherine Ramsland during her writing of *Piercing the Darkness*. The following is his story and personal involvement in making sure the vampire community remains a safe environment for everyone.

O'Mallie, a New York native, quickly found himself questioning the "norm". Interests peaked in the occult studies by the age of thirteen, and at the age of twenty-five Stephen became an essential element, with title, to this New York scene. Stephen began as one of the first Ronins in the scene, quickly establishing himself and his house. Throughout Stephen's twelve years in the scene, he sired many notable figures, who have gone on to establish their own houses. Co-founding House Vengeance, Stephen has as well continued to contribute to the scene. Now with over a decade in the scene and six years in law enforcement, Stephen comes out of the shadows with hopes of reviving the scene he holds close.

As a young adult interacting with others over the web, Stephen was introduced to this vampyre subculture. Invited behind the black veil, he soon found his place in the scene. Originally adopted by Father Vincent and Lady Sage, he became part of their private house. In his experience in this house, he found a sense of unity, familial ties, and loyal friendships. Becoming protective over his bloodline and the overall sense of acceptance, he moved on to establish his own house, the first protectorate house of Gotham, Clan O'Mallie. This clan soon became one of the most respected throughout the entire subculture.

Clan O'Mallie spanning over six years would eventually become a legacy house, siring no more children due to the change in location and conditions of the scene. This change made way for House Vengeance, a private house, to establish its name and with Stephen and the air to his throne Sean Sinner O'Mallie, as its founding fathers. Changes in the scene became vast with the siring of irresponsible and dishonest members; the true members soon went deeper underground. With the quick but drastic changes many original members lost touch and lost their desire to participate it what use to be a lifestyle that felt comfortable to them. With responsibilities of a career in law enforcement and a family Stephen became more removed from the scene. With many hopes and a strong desire to reconnect old friendships and revive a lifestyle and culture he grew up in, Stephen O'Mallie is stepping out of the shadows. As Co-Founders to House Vengeance Stephen and Sinner plan to give to their house what was given to them. This is a culture built on respect, loyalty, and an overall way to escape life's stresses and unwind. With a successful career as a homicide detective Stephen plans on changing stereotypes, educating the ignorant, and protecting the Night.

Underneath this thin veneer of poise lay predators. Some have no ethics and prey upon the unwary; deeming it their right to use anyone like a "living" battery and discard when drained. Fortunately, others feed from ambient energy in clubs and concerts or from consensual donors; harming no one. They follow The Black Veil and cling to manners in an effort to dislodge the stereotype of malice that folklore and modern fiction portrays of them. Clubs of a BDSM nature or large raves have been shut down by authorities, under the pretense of prostitution or drug raids because society fears what it does not understand. Some Pagans buy into the same hype and fear, treating Satanists and Vampires in a similar fashion as some of the Christians throughout history reacted to them, short of killing them! An ironic double standard. There are some who even belong to vampire churches. The Church of Satan is as equally protected as Wicca is in the U.S. Army guidebook, but it does not seem to matter. To protect our image, dark pagans, Goths, etc. either behave perfectly to prove false their unwarranted harassment, or lash out without any code of proper conduct.

Michelle Belanger's *Psychic Vampire Codex* explained clearly the types of Vampires that walk among us and ethically details both feeding techniques and conduct. My own book, *Embracing the Darkness; Understanding Dark Subcultures* explained away misconceptions many groups face in their own words, the feelings and reasons for being misunderstood from a plethora of individuals in hopes the mainstream would fear us less. But more importantly, we both strive to provide a voice for our peers, and offer guidance we didn't have.

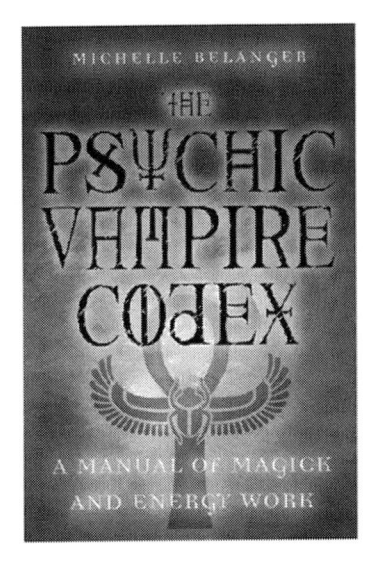

True predators exist in all classes of people, from doctors and lawyers in our everyday life to punks on the street. Just because the modern vampire happens to feel comfortable in an archetypical presentation publicly does not a monster make. It is unfortunate that the shadow side of life is full of many egomaniacs who believe their path condones rudeness, and malicious or unethical behavior. But it is the individuals' choice, not the type of lifestyle that dictates such things. The "asshole effect", as author John J. Coughlin calls it, of many in the left hand path who selfishly disregard the responsibility that power and leadership demand. One must strive to serve while leading, becoming an example. That is the role of an Elder, High Priest, or Dominate.

The best defense against attacks is to leave no chinks in your own armor Keeping a good reputation is vital and should be guarded carefully as one seldom gets the chance to earn respect twice in life. By acting noble, you inspire confidence. The words we use are weapons in the war of wills. People judge you by it as much as they do your choice of dress. There is power in a good vocabulary; it speaks of good breeding, manners, and intelligence.

If you wish to be treated like a king, act like a king. It has been said "For to princes and other great men, it is a rule to rule themselves that rule others." Ambition is a fine thing, and craving the finer things or power is not evil, but how it is gained, and how it is wielded is important. I am an elitist who wants to have the best in life. But I remember how hard the climb was and who helped me get there.

Tread lightly in the dark; you never know who you step on!

Allure of the Vampire by Corvis Nocturnum

Afterword

Vampires are exiles, excluded from society, light and warmth. Banished into the darkness, they thrive to this day enjoying modern urban life, devoid of dangers mere mortals face. Instead, it represents excitement, freedom, and gives them limitless possibilities. Vampires have gone from being the ultimate predator to being the ultimate outlaw. From what was once terrifying; to alluring. Instead of fleeing from him, we are drawn to him because we want to be like him, complete with the freedom from rules and social restrictions, all the way to the unrestrained nature of their sexuality. People look for the perfect mate and vampires seem to fit the role, especially for women. They want the perfect balance of a man, one who is both dark and mysterious; the bad boy who is daring, seductive and suave, but yet has the positive traits of being sensual, protective and usually wealthy. They are linked together with their offspring or lovers for an eternity, feeding into the fantasy of never being abandoned.

Vampires during all ages reflect us, and our society which is in perpetual turmoil from one issue of morality or another. No matter our age or personal sexual orientation, all people, all cultures have always had a love affair with the vampire. Classically, *Dracula* represented Victorian ideas, and decades later, we see a comparison with the angst of vampires in fiction mirroring from the days of gay bashing to clashing with so called "traditional family values," in Rice's book *Interview with the Vampire*.

We aren't afraid of monsters hiding the dark; we're afraid of ourselves, and vampires are exciting because they are the monsters so close to being us, because in most cases they *were* human. So close is the fantasy to our reality, is it any wonder the vampire has never lost its appeal.

For the last few two hundred years or so, from *Dracula* to *Twilight*, we have seen with the collective pop culture obsession over vampires being driven to a fever pitch. Societies do seem to go through various peaks of vampire frenzy, but this has been a particularly intense couple of years, and I think that's the nature of the vampire obsession.

When unsatisfied with our waking day life, we seek the shadows for the vampire mystique, their mastery over death and the power of blood vampirism can't help but brings us to them, even if it is in fantasy. Our collective obsession with sex and desire in our avoidance of death leads us to a natural conclusion, forever ensnaring us in the embrace of the vampire.

About the Author

Occult researcher and Gothic fantasy artist Corvis Nocturnum has owned an occult shop for several years while he maintained office as the Vice President of the Fort Wayne Pagan Alliance, a faith tolerance organization and acted as Vendor Director/Coordinator for Pagan Pride Day in Fort Wayne, Indiana. He has done lectures at various events all over Indiana, Ohio, and Illinois on the subjects in *Embracing the Darkness; Understanding Dark Subcultures,* work detailing the truth and crossover of alternative lifestyles, gaining the attention of readers all over the world. The grand and great-grandson of a Mason belongs to the Church of Satan, where he holds the second degree title of Warlock. He remains involved in bringing about public awareness to Satanism's true nature at conventions and universities, by being an invited speaker at a World Religions Seminar at the Indiana-Purdue University Fort Wayne where he enlightened the gathered individuals about Satanism. He has also been a repeated guest of Dr. Ed Craft on Magick Mind Radio. He was interviewed on Esoteric Radio in January of 2009. He has been an active voice in many dark communities, promoting public awareness on various issues, such as ethics, and explaining away misguided stereotypes. Various writings of his have appeared in newsletters and online groups, and he is currently the publisher of Dark Moon Press and of The Ninth Gate Magazine, a publication featuring fashion and interviews with bands in the Pagan, Satanic, Goth and Vampire communities. He serves as administrator on The Lost Children of the Oubliette, is a member of the Tantric Vampires forum, the Vampirism & Energy Work Research forum, and is also a member of the Voices of the Vampire Community (VVC). He also is co founder of the brick and mortar store, The Ninth Gate, located in Fort Wayne, Indiana. He is a May 2009 graduate with distinction from Brown Mackie College with an Associates degree who has made the Dean's List and Honors List several times. In his free time Corvis enjoys creating works of fantasy, pagan, and gothic artwork. He enjoys oil painting most of all. He continues to challenge himself not just artistically but also in the literary world with new writings. He is currently working on new books including some possible fiction.

Corvis Nocturnum can be reached for questions and appearances at:

corvisnocturnum@corvisnocturnum.com or to written mail via P.O. Box 11496, Fort Wayne, IN 46858.

Allure of the Vampire by Corvis Nocturnum

Appendices

Suggested Reading

The Vampire Library is a resource for readers of vampire fiction, literature and non-fiction books. This site offers lists of vampire books, detailed book information, and links to purchasing information where available. In association with Amazon.com.

Vampire Library, 1998-2008
http://www.vampirelibrary.com

Non Fiction Works
Reference

Complete Book of Vampires, Ghosts, & Poltergeists by Leonard R. N. Ashley

The Complete Vampire Companion by Rosemary Ellen Guiley and J. B. MacAbre

The Dracula Cookbook of Blood by Ardin C. Price

Northern Shadows: An Illustrated Guide to Canadian Vampires by John Arkelian

Treatise on Vampires and Revenants by Dom Augustine Calmet

V Is for Vampire: An A to Z Guide to Everything Undead by David J. Skal

Vampire: The Complete Guide to the World of the Undead by Manuela Dunn-Mascetti

The Vampire Book: The Complete Encyclopedia of the Undead by J. Gordon Melton

The Vampire Encyclopedia by Matthew E. Bunson

The Vampire Gallery by J. Gordon Melton

Vampires: Restless Creatures of the Night by Jean Marigny, translated by Lory Frankel

Dracula

Bram Stoker's Dracula: Sucking Through the Century edited by Carol Margaret Davison and Paul Simpson-Housley

Bram Stoker's Dracula: The Film and the Legend by James V. Hart

Dracula by Elizabeth Miller

The Dracula Book by Donald Glut

Dracula: Between Tradition and Modernism by Carol A. Senf

Dracula: Bram Stoker (New Casebooks) by Glennis Byron

Dracula: Prince of Many Faces by Radu R. Florescu & Raymond T. McNally

Dracula: Sense & Nonsense by Elizabeth Miller

Dracula: The Connoisseur's Guide by Leonard Wolf
Dracula: The First Hundred Years by Bob Madison
Dracula: The Novel and the Legend by Clive Leatherdale
Dracula: The Shade and the Shadow edited by Elizabeth Miller
Dracula: The Vampire & the Critics by Margaret L. Carter
Dracula: The Vampire Legend on Film by Robert Marrero
Dracula, Prince of Darkness by Martin H. Greenberg
Dracula in the Dark by James Craig Holte
Dracula Unearthed edited by Clive Leatherdale
The Essential Dracula by Leonard Wolf
In Search of Dracula: The History of Dracula and Vampires by Raymond T. McNally and Radu Florescu

The Origins of Dracula edited by Clive Leatherdale
Vlad III Dracula: The Life and Times of the Historical Dracula by Kurt W. Treptow

Anne Rice (Twayne's United States Authors) by Bette B. Roberts
Anne Rice: A Critical Companion by Jennifer Smith
Anne Rice: A Reader's Checklist and Reference Guide
The Anne Rice Reader edited by Katherine Ramsland
The Anne Rice Trivia Book by Katherine Ramsland
Conversations with Anne Rice by Michael Riley
The Gothic World of Anne Rice edited by Gary Hoppenstand & Ray B. Browne

Prism of the Night: A Biography of Anne Rice by Katherine Ramsland

The Vampire Companion by Katherine Ramsland

Vampires in Literature

Blood and Roses: Vampires in 19th Century Literature edited by Adele O. Gladwell

The Blood is the Life: Vampires in Literature edited by Leonard G. Heldreth & Mary Pharr

Blood Read edited by Joan Gordon, Veronica Hollinger & Brian W. Aldiss

Living Dead: A Study of the Vampire in Romantic Literature by James B. Twitchell

The Quotable Vampire edited by David Proctor

Reading the Vampire by Ken Gelder

The Vampire in Literature: A Critical Bibliography by Margaret L. Carter and Robert Scholes

The Vampire Omnibus edited by Peter Haining

Vampire Readings: An Annotated Bibliography by Patricia Altner

Vampires: Encounters with the Undead by David J. Skal

Vampyres: Lord Byron to Count Dracula by Christopher Frayling

Vampires on Film

Bram Stoker's Dracula: The Film and the Legend by James V. Hart & Francis Ford Coppola

Dracula: The Vampire Legend on Film by Robert Marrero

The Ingrid Pitt Bedside Companion for Vampire Lovers by Ingird Pitt

The Quotable Vampire edited by David Proctor

Reading the Vampire by Ken Gelder

The Vampire Film by Alain Silver & James Ursini

The Vampire Omnibus edited by Peter Haining

VideoHound's Vampires on Video by J. Gordon Melton

Myth and Reality

Allure of the Vampire; Our Sexual Attraction to the Undead by Corvis Nocturnum

Bloody Irish by Bob Curran

Children of the Night by Tony Thorne

Countess Dracula by Tony Thorne

Do Vampires Exist?

The Embrace: A True Vampire Story by Aphrodite Jones

Embracing the Darkness; Understanding Dark Subcultures by Corvis Nocturnum

Food for the Dead by Michael E. Bell

Forests of the Vampires: Slavic Myth

Liquid Dreams of Vampires by Martin V. Riccardo

Piercing the Darkness by Katherine Ramsland

Private Files of a Vampirologist: Case Histories & Letters edited by Jeanne K. Youngson

Real Vampires by Daniel Cohen

Something in the Blood by Jeff Guinn and Andy Grieser

Transformations edited by Time-Life Books & Jim Hicks

V Special Edition by Father Sebastian, Michelle Belanger and Layil Umbralux

The Vampire: In Legend & Fact by Basil Copper

The Vampire in Europe: True Tales of the Undead by Montague Summers

The Vampire Lectures by Laurence A. Rickels

The Vampire of Tradition: A Casebook edited by Alan Dundes

Vampires: The Occult Truth by Konstantinos

Vampires, Burial & Death: Folklore & Reality by Paul Barber

Vampires Among Us by Rosemary Ellen Guiley

Vampires and Vampirism: Legends from Around the World by Dudley Wright

Vampires or Gods? by William Meyers

Vampire Nation by Renee Russo

Fiction Series

American Vampire edited by Martin H. Greenberg and Lawrence Schimel

Anita Blake Vampire Hunter by Laurell K. Hamilton

Anno Dracula by Kim Newman

The Argeneau Series by Lynsay Sands

The Austra Family Series by Elaine Bergstrom

Allure of the Vampire by Corvis Nocturnum

The Black Dagger Brotherhood by J.R. Ward
Blood Ties by Jennifer Armintrout
Buffy the Vampire Slayer Novels

The Calling by Caridad Pineiro
Casa Dracula Series by Marta Acosta
The Children of the Dragon Series by T.M. Moore
Dante Valentine by Lilith Saintcrow
Dark Series (The Carpathians) by Christine Feehan
The Dark Ones Series by Katie MacAlister
Dark-Hunter Novels by Sherrilyn Kenyon
The Darkangel Trilogy by Meredith Ann Pierce
The Diaries of the Family Dracul by Jeanne Kalogridis
The Erotic Vampire Series edited by Cecilia Tan
The Eternity Series by Jayme Evans

The Gardella Vampire Chronicles by Colleen Gleason

The House of Night Series by P.C. and Kristin Cast
The Immortals After Dark Series by Kresley Cole

Jaz Parks by Jennifer Rardin
Jonathan Barrett by P.N. Elrod

Laws of the Blood by Susan Sizemore
The Lawson Vampire Novels by Jon F. Merz
Lee Nez Novels by Aimee and David Thurlo

The Mackenzie Vampire Series by Nina Bangs
The Mercy Thompson Series by Patricia Briggs
Midnight Romance Series by Nancy Gideon
The Moral Vampire Series by Rosemarie E. Bishop
The Morganville Vampires by Rachel Caine

The Necroscope Saga by Brian Lumley
New Tales of the Vampires by Anne Rice
Night World Series by L.J. Smith
The Noble Dead Saga by Barb and J.C. Hendee
Nosferatu Chronicles by Mick Farren

The Olivia Series by Chelsea Quinn Yarbro

Power of the Blood series by Nancy Kilpatrick
Primes by Susan Sizemore

The Rachel Morgan Series by Kim Harrison
Ravenloft Books
Regency Vampire Novels by Susan Squires

Saberhagen's Dracula by Fred Saberhagen

The Saga of Darren Shan by Darren Shan

The Saint-Germain Chronicles by Chelsea Quinn Yarbro

The Shadow Saga by Christopher Golden

Sisters of the Night by Chelsea Quinn Yarbro

The Southern Vampire Series by Charlaine Harris

The Tremayne Vampire Series by Linda Lael Miller

The Twilight Saga by Stephenie Meyer

The Undead Series by Mary Janice Davidson

The Vampire by Michael Romkey

Vampire: the Masquerade fiction from White Wolf Publishing

Vampire Academy by Richelle Mead

The Vampire Babylon Trilogy by Chris Marie Green

The Vampire Chronicles by Anne Rice

The Vampire Diaries by L.J. Smith

The Vampire Files by P.N. Elrod

Vampire Huntress Legends by L.A. Banks

Vampire Kisses by Ellen Schreiber

Vampire Legacy by Karen E. Taylor

The Vampire Saga by G.L. Giles

The Vampyricon by Douglas Clegg

Victoria Nelson Series by Tanya Huff

Wings in the Night by Maggie Shayne

Blood and Roses: Vampires in 19th Century Literature edited by Adele O. Gladwell

Blood Kiss: Vampire Erotica edited by Cecilia Tan

Blood Lines: Vampire Stories from New England edited by Martin H. Greenberg

Blood Thirst: 100 Years of Vampire Fiction edited by Leonard Wolf

Bloody Kisses A Vampire Anthology, Dark Moon Press

Bloody Irish by Bob Curran

Brothers of the Night: Gay Vampire Stories edited by Michael Rowe & Thomas S. Roche

Celebrity Vampires edited by Martin H. Greenberg

Cherished Blood: Vampire Erotica edited by Cecilia Tan

Classic Vampire Stories edited by Leslie Shepard

Classic Vampire Stories: Timeless Tales to Sink Your Teeth Into edited by Molly Cooper

A Coven of Vampires by Brian Lumley

Dark Angels: Lesbian Vampire Stories edited by Pam Keesey

The Darkest Thirst: A Vampire Anthology edited by Thomas J. Strauch

Daughters of Darkness: Lesbian Vampire Stories edited by Pam Keesey

Dead Brides: Vampire Tales by Edgar Allan Poe

The Dracula Book of Great Vampire Stories edited Leslie Shepard

Dracula in London edited by P.N. Elrod

Epiphanies of Blood by Bill Congreve

Erotica Vampirica: Sensual Vampire Stories edited by Cecilia Tan

Fields of Blood: Vampire Stories from the American Midwest edited by Martin H. Greenberg

Isaac Asimov's Vampires edited by Gardner Dozois & Sheila Williams

Highland Vampire by Hannah Howell, Adrienne Basso, Deborah Raleigh

His Immortal Embrace by Hannah Howell, Lynsay Sands, Sara Blayne, Kate Huntington

The Hunter's Prey by Diane Whiteside

The Kiss of Death: An Anthology of Vampire Stories edited by Thomas J. Strauch

Love in Vein edited by Poppy Z. Brite

Love in Vein II edited by Poppy Z. Brite & Martin H. Greenberg

Mammoth Book of Dracula: Vampire Tales for the New Millennium edited by Stephen Jones

Mammoth Book of Vampire Stories by Women edited by Stephen Jones

Mammoth Book of Vampires edited by Stephen Jones

Masters of Midnight by Michael Thomas Ford

Midnight Garden: A Vampire Collection by K.R. McGee

Midnight Mass edited by Martin H. Greenberg

Night Bites: Vampire Stories by Women edited by Victoria A. Brownworth

Penguin Book of Vampire Stories edited by Alan Ryan

Sisters of the Night edited by Barbara Hambly and Martin H. Greenberg

Sons of Darkness edited by Michael Rowe & Thomas S. Roche

Southern Blood: Vampire Stories from the American South edited by Martin H. Greenberg

Streets of Blood: Vampire Stories from New York City edited by Martin H. Greenberg

The Time of the Vampires edited by P.N. Elrod and Martin H. Greenberg

The Ultimate Dracula edited by Byron Preiss

Vampire Detectives edited by Martin H. Greenberg
The Vampire Omnibus edited by Peter Haining
Vampire Slayers edited by Martin H. Greenberg & Elizabeth Ann Scarborough
Vampire Stories edited by Richard Dalby
The Vampire Stories of Nancy Kilpatrick by Nancy Kilpatrick
Vampire Stories of R. Chetwynd-Hayes edited by Stephen Jones
Vampires: Encounters with the Undead edited by David J. Skall
Vampires: The Greatest Stories edited by Martin H. Greenberg

A Whisper of Blood edited by Ellen Datlow

Individual Novels and Sequels
Absence of Faith by E. Carter Jones
After Midnight stories by Carol Finch, Colleen Faulkner and Karen Ranney
After Twilight by Amanda Ashley, Christine Feehan and Ronda Thompson
Alexandru: A Vampire's Legacy Continues by Rebecca K. Rhodes
Ancestral Hungers by Scott Baker

Batman and Dracula by Doug Moench
Beneath a Blood Red Moon by Shannon Drake

Bite by Richard Laymon

Black Rush by Frederick Louis Richardson

Blood: The Last Vampire 2002 by Benkyo Tamaoki

Blood and Chrysanthemums by Nancy Baker

Blood Bond by Suzy Miner

Blood Covenant by Mary Lamb

Blood Feud by Sam Siciliano

Blood Dreaming: A Collection of Gothic Ku by Lewis Sanders

Blood is Thicker Than Water by Wynette A. Hoffman

Blood Legacy: The Novel by Kerri Hawkins

The Blood of the Covenant by Brent Monahan

The Blood of the Goddess by William Schindler

Blood Memories by Barb Hendee

Blood Red: A Vampires Love Story by J.C. Brinson-Untiet

Blood Road by Edo Van Belkom

Blood Tears by Raven Dane

Blood to Blood by Elaine Bergstrom

Blood Walk by Lee Killough

Blood Will Tell by Jean Lorrah

Bloodshift by Garfield Reeves-Stevens

Bloodsong by Karen Marie Christa Minns

Bloodsucking Fiends by Christopher Moore

BloodWind by Charlotte Boyett-Compo

Blue Bloods by Melissa De La Cruz

Blythe: NightVision by David Quinn, Hannibal King

The Book of Common Dread by Brent Monahan
The Book of the Dark by William Meikle
Bound in Blood by David Thomas Lord
Bring on the Night by Don & Jay Davis
The Burning by Susan Squires

Candle Bay by Tamara Thorne
Carmilla by J. Sheridan Le Fanu
Carmilla: The Return by Kyle Marffin
Cathedral of Vampires by Mary Ann Mitchell
Children of the Night by Dan Simmons
Children of the Night by Mercedes Lackey
Come the Night by Angelique Armae
Companions of the Night by Vivian Vande Velde
The Cowboy and the Vampire by Clark Hays and Kathleen McFaul
Crimson Dreams by Margaret L. Carter
Crimson Kiss by Trisha Baker
Crimson Night by Trisha Baker
Crimson Shadows by Trisha Baker
Curse of the Vampire by David A. Wilson

Dance with the Dragon by E.F. Watkins
Dancing with the Devil by Keri Arthur
The Dark Blood of Poppies by Freda Warrington

Dark Changeling by Margaret L. Carter

Dark Dreams by Jane Harrison

Dark Hunger by Mayra Calvani

Dark Rapture by Michele Hauf

Dark Salvation by Jennifer Dunne

A Darker Dream by Amanda Ashley

Darkhour Vampires: Captivity by Linda Suzane

Darkness on the Ice by Lois Tilton

The Darkness Therein by Kate Hill

Darkspawn by Lois Tilton

Daughter of Darkness by Steven Spruill

Daughters of the Moon by Joseph Curtin

Dawn of the Vampire by William Hill

Dead Walkers: The Protectorate by Angelique Armae

Deadly Obsession by Patricia A. Rasey

Deep Is the Night: Dark Fire by Denise A. Agnew

Deep Is the Night: Night Watch by Denise A. Agnew

Deep Midnight by Shannon Drake

Deeper than the Night by Amanda Ashley

The Delicate Dependency by Michael Talbot

Demon in My View by Amelia Atwater-Rhodes

Desires Unleashed by D.N. Simmons

Desmodus by Melanie Tem

Desmond by Ulysses G. Dietz

Dracul: An Eternal Love Story by Nancy Kilpatrick

Allure of the Vampire by Corvis Nocturnum

Dracul: The Vampire Returns by James C. Wardlaw
Dracula by Bram Stoker
Dracula the Undead by Freda Warrington
Dracula: A Symphony in Moonlight & Nightmares Jon J. Muth
Dracula's Tomb by Colin McNaughton

Embrace the Night by Amanda Ashley
Enemy Mine by Jewell Dart
The Eternal Battle by Keith Gouveia
Eternally Yours by S. L. Juers

Facade of Shadows by Rick Chiantaretto
Fiery Roses by Lorena Glass
Fledgling: A Novel by Octavia E. Butler
The Flesh, the Blood and the Fire by S. A. Swiniarski
Full Moon Inheritance by Jacqueline Elliott
Full Moon Rising by Keri Arthur

Galen by Allan Gilbreath
A Gift of Blood by JennaKay Francis
The Gilda Stories: A Novel by Jewelle Gomez
Gothique by Kyle Marffin
The Guardian by Beecher Smith
The Guilty Innocent: Knight of the Darkness Book Two by D.N. Simmons

H.M.S. Vanguard: A Tale of Horror by John Conrad

Hawkes Harbor by S.E. Hinton

The Heat Seekers by Katherine Ramsland

His Father's Son by Nigel Bennett and P.N. Elrod

The Historian by Elizabeth Kostova

The Hour Before Dawn by Patricia A. Rasey

How to Marry a Millionaire Vampire by Kerrelyn Sparks

The Hunger by Whitley Strieber

I Am Dracula by C. Dean Andersson

I Am Legend by Richard Burton Matheson

I.M. Internet Message by Stephanie Simpson-Woods

The Immaculate by Kate Hill

In the Forests of the Night by Amelia Atwater-Rhodes

Insatiable by David Dvorkin

Internal Anomaly by C. L. Hunter

J's Atonement by Jessie A. Snow

Keeper of the King by Nigel Bennett and P.N. Elrod

Kiss of the Vampire by Nancy Baker (a.k.a *The Night Inside*)

Knights of the Darkness: Book One of the Slayer Archives by Nick Lewis

Lacroix by Ardella Reliford

The Last Vampire by Whitley Strieber

The Last Vampire by T.M. Wright

The Letters of Mina Harker by Dodie Bellamy

Lilith's Dream by Whitley Strieber

The London Vampire Panic by Michael Romkey

Look for Me by Moonlight by Mary Downing Hahn

Lord of the Dead by Tom Holland

Lost Souls by Poppy Z. Brite

Love Bite by Sherry Gottleib

Love in the Dark by Christien Churchill

Madonna of the Dark by Elaine Moore

Masquerade by Melissa De La Cruz

Midnight Embrace by Amanda Ashley

Midnight Mass by F. Paul Wilson

Midnight Predator by Amelia Atwater-Rhodes

Mina: The Dracula Story Continues by Marie Kiraly

Monastery by Patrick Whalen

My Demon's Kiss (Bound in Darkness) by Lucy Blue

Never Ceese by Sue Dent

... never dream by Scott Charles Adams

The Night Inside by Nancy Baker (a.k.a. *Kiss of the Vampire*)

Night of the Dragon's Blood by William Pridgen

Night of the Harvest Moon by Everett L. Winrow

Night Players by P.D. Cacek

Night Pleasures by Sherrilyn Kenyon

Night Prayers: A Vampire Story by P.D. Cacek

Night Thirst by Patrick Whalen

Nightchild: A Clans Novel by J.A. Cummings

No Release: A Vampire's Tale by Elaina Harper

Nocturnas by Shawn Ryan

Nosferatu: A Novel by Jim Shepard

The Nymphos of Rocky Flats: A Novel by Mario Acevedo

Of Elves and Vampires: Trinity's Mark by Ella Scopilo

One Foot in the Grave by Wm. Mark Simmons

One With the Hunger by J. C. Wilder

Pandora's Game by Christopher Andrews

Past Sins by Don Ecker

Prince of Misery by Heather Crews

Prince of the Night by Jasmine Cresswell

Prince of Dreams by Susan Krinard

Puncture by Lisa V. Proulx

Quenched by Mary Ann Mitchell

Quincy Morris, Vampire by P.N. Elrod

Raga Six by Frank Lauria
Rapture in Moonlight by Rosemary Laurey
Raven by S.A. Swiniarski
Realm of Shadows by Shannon Drake
Red Moon Rising by Billie Sue Mosiman
Reflections of a Vampire by Damion Kirk
Renfield: A Tale of Madness by Kyle Garrett and Galen Showman
The Ruby Tear Rebecca Brand
Rulers of Darkness by Steven Spruill

Salem's Lot by Stephen King
Sealed in Blood by Margaret L. Carter
Shades of Gray by Amanda Ashley
The Shadow of the Succubus/The Eternal Thirst by John Condenzio
Shadow of the Vampuss by Karen Mahony and Alex Ukolov
Shadow's Embrace by Astrid Cooper
Shadows After Dark by Ouida Crozier
Shadows Bite by Stephen Dedman
Shards of Faith by Heather Lee Fleming
Shattered Mirror by Amelia Atwater-Rhodes
The Silver Kiss by Annette Curtis Klause
Sips of Blood by Mary Ann Mitchell
Slave of My Thirst by Tom Holland

Slayer by Karen Koehler
Slayer: Black Miracles by Karen Koehler
Sorrow: A Vampire's Tale by J.W. James
Soul of the Vampire by Minda Samiels
The Soulless by L.G. Burbank
The Stake by Richard Laymon
Strangers in the Night stories by Anne Stuart, Chelsea Quinn Yarbro & Maggie Shayne
The Summoning by Bentley Little
The Sun Will Find You by Chris Muffoletto
Sunlight Moonlight by Amanda Ashley
Sunshine by Robin McKinley

Tainted Blood by Mary Ann Mitchell
A Taste for Blood by Diana Lee
A Taste of Blood Wine by Freda Warrington
Tepes by Johann Wolfe Heisey
Templar's Fire by Larry Schliessmann
A Terrible Beauty by Nancy Baker
They Thirst by Robert McCammon
Thirst by Michael Cecilione
Thirst by Pyotyr Kurtinski
Thirsty by M.T. Anderson
A Thorned Rose by J.L. Ault
Those Who Hunt the Night by Barbara Hambly

Touch of Evil by C. T. Adams, Cathy Clamp
Touch the Dark by Karen Chance
Traveling With the Dead by Barbara Hambly
Turnbull Bay by Liberty
Twilight Healer by Barbara Custer
Twilight Hour by Brad Lawson

Unexpected Unexplained: Vampires by Kristie Lynn Higgins
Unholy Penance by Roberta Ideus
Unholy Thirst by Richard Long and Terry Allen

Vampire: 1989 by Brett A. Contreras
The Vampire Apocalypse: Books One: Revelations by Katriena Knights
Vampire Apocalypse: A World Torn Asunder by Derek Gunn
Vampire City by Paul Feval
Vampire Cheetah by Sheila Lee
The Vampire Hunters by William Hill
The Vampire Journals by Traci Briery
Vampire Junction by S.P. Somtow
The Vampire Memoirs by Traci Briery
Vampire Nation by Thomas M. Sipos
Vampire Royalty: The Rebellion by Valerie Hoffman
Vampire Slayer: One Foot in Darkness by Dani A. Camden
The Vampire Tapestry by Suzy McKee Charnas

The Vampire Viscount by Karen Harbaugh

Vampire Vow by Michael Schiefelbein

Vampire Winter by Lois Tilton

The Vampire Within: The Beginning by Drew Silver

The Vampire's Beautiful Daughter by S.P. Somtow

The Vampire's Kiss by Cynthia Eden

The Vampire's Violin by Michael Romkey

Vampire's Waltz by Thomas Staab

Vampire$ by John Steakley

Vampires & Chocolates by Greg Shelton

Vampires of the Scarlet Order by David Lee Summers

The Vampyre by John Polidori

A Vampyre's Blues by Chris Hayden

Vampyrrhic by Simon Clark

Vanitas: Escape from Vampire Junction by S.P. Somtow

Vegas Vampires by William Hill

The Very Bloody Marys by M. Christian

Vlad Dracula: The Dragon Prince by Michael Augustyn

Vrolok by Nolene-Patricia Dougan

The Wages of Sin by Jenna Maclaine

Walk in Moonlight by Rosemary Laurey

Watchers: The Battle for the Throne by William Meikle

Watchers: The Coming of the King by William Meikle

Watchers of the Wall by William Meikle

What Big Teeth You Have: A Vampire Tale by Jimmy Autrey

When Darkness Falls by Shannon Drake

Wicked Angels by Michele Hauf

A Willful Taste by Willa Okati

Worse than Death by Sherry Gottleib

X-Rated Bloodsuckers by Mario Acevedo

Yellow Fog by Les Daniels

Suggested Viewing

Vampire of the Coast (1909)

The Vampire's Trail (1910)

The Vampire (1913)--Kalem film directed by Robert Vignola.

In the Grip of the Vampire (1913)

Vampires of the Night (1914)--Greene's Feature Photo Plays.

The Vampire's Trail (1914)--directed by Robert Vignola.

Vampires of Warsaw (1914)

The Vampire's Tower (1914)--Ambrosia film.

Saved From the Vampire (1914)

The Devil's Daughter (1915)

A Fool There Was (1915)--Theda Bara as predatory "Vamp."

The Vampire's Clutch (1915)--Knight film.

Was She A Vampire? (1915)--Universal film.

Kiss of the Vampire (1915)

Mr. Vampire (1916)

A Night of Horror (1916)--German film directed by Arthur Robison.

A Vampire Out of Work (1916)--Vitagraph film.

A Village Vampire (1916)

The Beloved Vampire (1917)

The Vampire (1920)--Metro film.

Drakula (1921)

The Blond Vampire (1922)

Nosferatu (1922)--German Max Schreck as Count Orlock; dir. F.W. Murnau.

London After Midnight (1927)--Lon Chaney as vampire in human disguise.

The Vampire (1928)--seducer, not undead.

Dracula (1931)--Bela Lugosi and balletic style of movement.

Vampyr (1932)--loose "Carmilla" adaptation by Danish director Dreyer.

The Vampire Bat (1933)--Lionel Atwill as mad doctor.

Mark of the Vampire (1935)--remake of 1927's London After Midnight.

Condemned to Live (1935)--baby of bitten woman becomes vampire/werewolf.

Dracula's Daughter (1936)--adaptation of Stoker's "Dracula's Guest."

House of Dark Shadows (1970)--Jonathan Frid as Barnabas Collins.

Count Dracula (1970)—ChristThe Devil Bat (1940)--Lugosi raises bats for revenge.

Spooks Run Wild (1941)--Lugosi as magician suspected of being vampire.

The Return of the Vampire (1943)--Bela Lugosi with different vampire name.

Son of Dracula (1943)--Lon Chaney, Jr. emigrates to the States.

Dead Men Walk (1943)--George Zucco as vampire.

Return of the Vampire (1943)--Lugosi as vampire in WWII England.

House of Frankenstein (1944)--John Carradine as the Count.

House of Dracula (1945)--John Carradine again.

Isle of the Dead (1945)--Karloff accuses girl.

The Vampire's Ghost (1945)--in a small African village.

The Devil Bat's Daughter (1946)--Daddy visits in sleep.

Abbott and Costello Meet Frankenstein (1948)--Lugosi as Dracula too.

Old Mother Riley Meets the Vampire (1948)--Lugosi in British comedy

The Thing From Another World (1951)--outer space blooddrinker on Earth.

The Devil's Commandment (1956)

The Vampire (1957)--accidental pill-taking leads to vampirism.

Blood of Dracula (1957)--a.k.a. Blood is My Heritage, Blood of the Demon.

Not of This Earth (1957)--Roger Corman combines sci-fi and vampirism.

The Return of Dracula (1957)--low-quality, a.k.a. The Curse of Dracula.

Horror of Dracula (1958)--Christopher Lee; Hammer Films.

Blood of the Vampire (1958)--anemic doctor victimizes

patients.

Curse of the Undead (1959)--cowboy theme.

The Vampire's Coffin (1958)--sequel to 1957's The Vampire.

Uncle Was a Vampire (1959)--Italian satire with Christopher Lee.

World of the Vampires (1960)--pipe-organ made with human bones.

Brides of Dracula (1960)--Oedipal Hammer film set in girls' boarding school.

Blood and Roses (1961)--Roger Vadim's adaptation of "Carmilla."

Black Sunday (1961)--Barbara Steele as vampire/witch in Italian film.

Sampson vs. the Vampire Women (1961)--Mexican wrestling hero Santo.

Bring Me the Vampire (1961)--Mexican inheritance comedy.

House on Bare Mountain (1962)--sexploitation with Frankenstein and Wolfman.

Kiss of the Vampire (1963)--honeymooners in Bavaria encounter cult.

The Last Man on Earth (1964)--Vincent Price after atomic holocaust.

Dr. Terror's House of Horrors (1964)--Peter Cushing is Death.

The Vampires (1964)--a.k.a. Goliath and the Vampires; Italian gladiator.

Dracula, Prince of Darkness (1965)--Christopher Lee; Hammer Films.

Planet of the Vampires (1965)--Italian sci-fi; crew turn into space vampires.

Devils of Darkness (1965)--modern-day victims from Brittany.

Blood Fiend (1966)--Christopher Lee as suspect.

The Vampire People (1966)--Filipino film with bald heart-thief.

Track of the Vampire (1966)--Roger Corman production of artist and wax death.

Billy the Kid vs. Dracula (1966)--outlaw-turned-hero terrorized.

Blood Bath (1966)--a.k.a. Track of the Vampire.

The Devil's Mistress (1966)

Planet of Blood (1966)--a.k.a. Queen of Blood; Corman, Basil Rathbone.

The Fearless Vampire Killers (1967)--Roman Polanski spoof with Sharon Tate.

A Taste of Blood (1967)--Dracula's descendant's revenge on descendants.

Dr. Terror's Gallery of Horror (1967)

Dracula's Wedding Day (1967)

Dracula Meets the Outer Space Chicks (1967)

Draculita (1967)

Dracula Has Risen From the Grave (1968)--Christopher Lee's third outing.

Mad Monster Party (1968)--stop-motion monsterfest.

The Blood of Dracula's Castle (1969)--"a poor film."

The Blood Beast Terror (1969)--British.

The Nude Vampire (1969)--French film with suicide cult in old castle.

Space Vampires (1969)--John Carradine; a.k.a. Astro-Zombies

Christopher Lee and Klaus Kinski; a shoddy production.

The Scars of Dracula (1970)--Christopher Lee stalking and drinking.

Taste the Blood of Dracula (1970)--Christopher Lee and hypocritical Victorians.

Count Yorga, The Vampire (1970)--East European in California.

The Devil's Skin (1970)

Dracula's Vampire Lust (1970)

The Vampire Lovers (1970)--Hammer with a "Carmilla" adaptation.

Blood of Frankenstein (1970)--Zandor Vorkov as the Count.

Dracula vs. Frankenstein (1970)--American version.

Lust For a Vampire (1970)--Hammer and "Carmilla" echoes.

Countess Dracula (1970)--Hammer with Ingrid Pitt as sadist.

Guess What Happened to Count Dracula (1970)--sexploitation.

The Return of Count Yorga (1971)--sequel to the 1970 film.

Vampire Men of the Lost Planet (1971)--astronauts sent to planet.

Nosferatu in Brazil (1971)--Portuguese 8mm spoof.

The Bloodsuckers (1971)--Greek devil-worship with Patrick MacNee.

The Vampire Happening (1971)--Transylvania inheritance spoof.

The Velvet Vampire (1971)--couple stranded in desert invited into home.

Daughters of Darkness (1971)

Lake of Dracula (1971)--a.k.a. Bloodthirsty Eyes, Japanese.

Blacula (1972)--Caribbean Count.

Dracula A.D. 1972 (1972)--Christopher Lee.

Saga of the Draculas (1972)--aging Count's interest in pregnant niece.

The Night Stalker (1972)

The Werewolf vs. The Vampire Woman (1972)--a.k.a. Shadow of the Werewolf.

Dracula in Brianza (1972)

Dracula's Great Love (1972)

The Deathmaster (1972)

The Legend of Blood Castle (1972)--17th-century Hungarian

nobleman.

Grave of the Vampire (1972)--baby drinks mom's blood from bottle.

Bram Stoker's Dracula (1973)--Jack Palance as Dracula; Dan Curtis Productions.

Scream, Blacula, Scream (1973)--Pam Grier's voodoo must send him back.

Satanic Rites of Dracula (1973)--Christopher Lee as CEO and germ warfare.

Andy Warhol's Dracula (1973)--Italian/French with aging Dracula.

The Daughter of Dracula (1973)

Dead People (1973)

Lemora: A Vampire's Tale (1973)--odyssey of teenager in the 1930s.

The Devil's Plaything (1973)

The Devil's Wedding Night (1973)

Old Dracula (1974)--David Niven.

Captain Kronos, Vampire Hunter (1974)--victims robbed of youth.

The Seven Brothers Meet Dracula (1974)--martial arts and Peter Cushing.

Evil of Dracula (1974)--Japanese sequel to 1971's Lake of Dracula.

Vampyres (1974)--two female hitchhikers.

Deafula (1975)

Dead of Night (1976)

Rabid (1977)--Marilyn Chambers has bloodsucking organ under arm.

Doctor Dracula (1977)

Dracula and Son (1977)--Christopher Lee's son wants to be a florist.

Dracula's Dog (1977)--a.k.a. Zoltan: Hound of Dracula.

Martin (1977)--George A. Romero directs film regarding guilt and morality.

Count Dracula (1978)--British tv with Louis Jourdan.

Dracula (1979)--Frank Langella and Laurence Olivier.

Vampire (1979)--San Francisco millionaire; produced by Bochco.

Dracula Blows His Cool (1979)

Nosferatu: The Vampire (1979)--Klaus Kinski in slow remake of 1922 film.

Thirst (1979)--descendant of Countess Bathory and secret society.

Love at First Bite (1979)--George Hamilton spoof with Susan Saint James.

Vampire Hookers (1979)--a.k.a. Night of the Bloodsuckers, with John Carradine.

Dracula Sucks (1979)--Jamie Gillis.

Salem's Lot: The Movie (1979)--originally 4-hour tv movie.

Dracula's Last Rites (1980)--vampire mortician.

Mama Dracula (1980)--Baroness Bathory spoof.

Deadline (1980)

Dr. Dracula (1981)

Dracula Rises From His Coffin (1982)

The Hunger (1983)--Catherine Deneuve, David Bowie, Susan Sarandon.

A Polish Vampire in Burbank (1984)--nerd vampire spoof.

Fright Night (1985)--kid and Roddy McDowall vs. neighbor.

Once Bitten (1985)--Lauren Hutton comedy.

The Seven Vampires (1985)--botanical chaos.

Dragon Against Vampire (1985)

Lifeforce (1985)--space expedition brings back trouble to London.

Vampire Hunter D (1985) -- Japanese anime novel.

Dracula, the Great Undead (1985) -- Documentary

Demon Queen (1986) -- Female vampire on bloody rampage.

Vamp (1986)--Grace Jones vs. college students.

The Devil Vendetta (1986)

Mr. Vampire (1986)--Hong Kong martial arts and slapstick.

The Lost Boys (1987)--bad influence of the gang.

The Monster Squad (1987)

Near Dark (1987)

I Married a Vampire (1987)--comedy with Brendan Hickey, Rachel Golden.

My Best Friend Is a Vampire (1988)--after last date, he likes rare hamburgers.

Love Bites (1988)--gay spoof.

Teen Vamp (1988)--high school nerd transformed.

Beverly Hills Vamp (1988)--California girls stay out of the sun.

Dance of the Damned (1988)

Dinner With the Vampire (1988)

Dracula's Widow (1988)

Vampire at Midnight (1988)--L.A. cop vs. vampire.

Because the Dawn (1988)--Lesbian vampires.

Nightlife (1989)

To Die For (1989)--Dracula in L.A.

Daughter of Darkness (1989)--she discovers in Romania dad was vampire.

Vampire's Kiss (1989)--Nicholas Cage paranoid about Jennifer Beals.

Rockula (1989)--300-year-old teen vampire in a musical spoof.

Fright Night: Part II (1989)--Roddy McDowall vs. female vampire.

Dawn (1990)

Sundown: Vampire in Retreat (1990)

Rockula (1990) -- A young vampire is cursed to stay a virgin.

Doctor Vampire (1991)

Blood Ties (1991)--made for tv.

Subspecies (1991)

Kingdom of the Vampire (1991)--Jeff vs. witchy mother.

Pale Blood (1991)--kinky L.A. tale of vampire looking for love.

Vampire Cop (1991)--night shift and tv reporter.

The Reflecting Skin (1991)--a Midwest boy's paranoia about widow next door.

Bram Stroker's Dracula (1992)--Gary Oldman; Francis Ford Coppola.

Innocent Blood (1992)

Children of the Night (1992)--Mother and daughter vampires emprisoned by priest.

Buffy, the Vampire Slayer (1992)

Tale of a Vampire (1992)

Dracula's Hair (1992)

Sleepwalkers (1992) -- Stephen King and Egyptology.

To Sleep With a Vampire (1992)--vampire with stripper seeking son.

My Grandpa Is a Vampire (1992)--Al Lewis from "The Munsters."

Darkness (1993)

Bloodstone: Subspecies II (1993)

Bloodlust: Subspecies III (1993)--vampire Radu, his mummy, and subspecies.

Love Bites (1993)--vampire hunter in love with prey.

Blood Ties (1993)

Dracula Rising (1993)

Tale of a Vampire (1993)--London library scholar searching for lost love.

To Sleep with a Vampire (1993)

Project Vampire (1993)--world domination (would end the food supply?).

Blood in the Night (1993)

City of the Vampires (1993)

Cronos (1993)--mechanized scarab inflicts vampirism.

Vampire Vixens From Venus (1994)--three alien drug smugglers.

Vampires and Other Stereotypes (1994)--detectives and chaos from Hell.

Demonsoul (1994)

Interview With the Vampire (1994)

Embrace of the Vampire (1995)--Alyssa Milano as tempted college student.

Vampire in Brooklyn (1995)

Dracula: Dead and Loving It (1995)

Addicted to Murder (1995)--Midwest boy meets vampire in the woods.

From Dusk 'Til Dawn (1996)

Bordello of Blood (1996)

Dead of Night (1996)

The Vampire Journals (1996)--Vengeful Vamp out to destroy line who turned him.

An American Vampire Story (1997)--New friends turn out to be bad vampires.

Def By Temptation (1997)--Samuel L. Jackson in erotic thriller.

Addicted to Murder: Tainted Blood (1998)--A rebel vampire converts unworthy victims.

Blade (1998)

John Carpenter's Vampires (1998)

Teenage Space Vampires (1998)--Aliens turn out to be a strange vampire species.

Addicted to Murder 3: Blood Lust (1999) -- Someone is feeding on vampire flesh.

Cold Hearts (1999) -- Two young women must kill to live.

The Vampire Carmilla (1999) -- Vampire stalks friends of her great-great-granddaughter.

Vampire Blues (1999) -- New Jersey teen vacations in Spain.

2000s:

Dark Prince: The True Story of Dracula (2000)

Dracula 2000 (2000) -- Count Dracula is once again unleashed upon the world.

Mom's Got a Date with a Vampire (2000) -- Made for TV.

Shadow of the Vampire (2000) -- The 1922 *Nosferatu* Schreck as a real vampire.

Blood (2000) -- Vampire's blood made genetically narcotic.

Vampires: Los Muertos (2001) -- Jon Bon, vampire hunter.

Jesus Christ, Vampire Hunter (2001) -- Jesus is called back to a harassed Ottawa.

Vampire Hunter D Bloodlust (2001) -- Japanese anime novel.

The Erotic Rites of Countess Dracula (2001) -- Female vampire rock star in the '60s.

The Forsaken (2001)

Blade II (2002)

Queen of the Damned (2002) -- Vaguely Anne Ricey.

Vampire Clan (2002) -- Those crazy homicidal teens.

An Erotic Vampire in Paris (2002) -- Lesbian Parisian adventure.

Barely Legal Lesbian Vampires (2003) -- Camilla courts Lilith.

Dracula II: Ascension (2003) -- Med students offered cash for ancient plasma.

Vampires Anonymous (2003) -- Vic the Vampire in a 12-step program.

Vlad (2003) -- Three American students in the Carpathian mountains.

Underworld (2003)

Vampires: Out for Blood (2004) -- Rave scene as feeding grounds.

Blood Angels (2004) -- Older sister is vampiric seductress.

Vampires vs. Zombies (2004) -- Infected girl and father encounter both.

Lust for Dracula (2004) -- Housewife and updated Stoker character names.

Vampire Sisters (2004) -- Adult entertainment web site by vampire prostitutes.

Dracula 3000 (2004) -- Transport vessel has been missing for a century.

Van Helsing (2004)

Vampires: The Turning (2005) -- Martial arts and Thai vampire hunters.

Bram Stoker's Way of the Vampire (2005)

Vampire Community Web Sites & Resources

Voices of the Vampire Community (VVC)
http://www.veritasvosliberabit.com/vvc.html

Sanguinarius Real Vampire Resource Site
http://www.sanguinarius.org

SphynxCat's Real Vampires Support Page
http://sphynxcatvp.nocturna.org

Suscitatio Enterprises, LLC Research Site
Vampirism & Energy Work Research Study
http://www.suscitatio.com

The Vampiric Community Message Board & Resource Site
http://www.vcmb.org

Darkness Embraced Vampire & Occult Society
http://www.darknessembraced.com

Psychic Vampire Resource Site & Forum
http://www.psychicvampire.org

Smoke & Mirrors Support Forum
http://smokeandmirrors34981.yuku.com

Smoke & Mirrors Dark Forum
http://www.smokenmirrorshome.com/phpBB3

House Kheperu Resource Site
http://www.kheperu.org

Atlanta Vampire Alliance [AVA] Resource Site & Forum
http://www.atlantavampirealliance.com

TrueForm Within Resource Site & Forum
http://www.trueformwithin.org

Drink Deeply & Dream Resource Site & Forum
http://www.drinkdeeplyanddream.com

By Light Unseen Resource Site
http://www.bylightunseen.net

The Vampire Church Resource Site & Forum
http://www.vampire-church.com

Shadowlore Resource Site & Forum

http://www.shadowlore.net

Les Vampires Resource Site & Yahoo Group
http://www.lesvampires.org

Vampires Realm Of Darkness Resource Site & Forum
http://www.vampires.nu

Lost Children Of The Oubliette
http://tlcoto.salemsloft.com

Black Swan Haven
http://www.blackswanhaven.org

The Vampirism Community eList Yahoo Group
http://groups.yahoo.com/group/vampirism

Vampire Nation Yahoo Group
http://groups.yahoo.com/group/Vampiresnest

Strigoi Vii (OSV) Current Of Elorath Forum
http://forum.sanguinarium.net/forums

Temple Of The Vampire
http://www.vampiretemple.com

Vampyre Support & Information Society
http://www.vsis.co.nr

Immortal Covenant Resource Site & Forum
http://www.immortalcovenant.com

Damn Society Dwelling Vampyres
http://www.dsdv.com

Nocturnus Online Resource Site & Forum
http://www.nocturnusonline.net

Nocturnal Voices Society Resource Site & Forum
http://www.nocturnalvoices.com

Temple United Vampyre Unitarian Pagan (UVUP) Forum
http://www.templeUVUP.com

From The Ashes Forum
http://risefromdeadashes.yuku.com

Vampgeist Resource Site
http://www.vampgeist.com

Darker Than Thou Resource Site & Forum

http://www.darkerthanthou.net

SangSpace Vampire Community
http://vampspace.ning.com

Tantric Vampires - A Psi-Sexual Vampire Community
http://tantricvampires.ning.com

Silken Shadows Vampire Community
http://ssvcgroup.ning.com

Fallen Creations Teen Vampire Community
http://fcvcgroup.ning.com

Vampress.net Resource Site & Forum
http://www.vampress.net

VTK Vampire/Goth/Fetish Resource Site & Forum
http://www.vampyres.tk

Vampire Rave Resource Site
http://www.vampirerave.com

Manerium Lamiis - French Forum
http://www.maneriumlamiis.net

Vampire at Eternal - French Forum
http://vampires.leforum.eu/portal.php

Sanctum du Lutetia (OSV) - French Forum
http://forum.vampyrisme.fr

PsiVamp.net - German Resource Site & Forum
http://www.psivamp.net

Vampyrs - German Forum
http://www.vampyrs.de

Vampyrbibliothek German Resource Site
http://www.vampyrbibliothek.de

Noctemeron - German Resource Site
http://www.noctemeron.de

Vampyrismo - Brazilian Resource Site & Forum
http://www.vampyrismo.org

Hadedes Khepra - Brazilian Forum
http://templovampirico.forumeiros.com

Into The Night - Czech Forum
http://vampyressupportsitemessageboard.yuku.com

Russian Vampire Resource Site
http://www.vampirizm.ru

Armenian Vampire Resource Site
http://realvampires.do.am

The Path of the Kherete
http://www.kherete.org

House Of The Dreaming - International
http://www.houseofthedreaming.net

House Quinotaur – International
http://www.house-quinotaur.org

House Sahjaza - New York City, NY
http://www.sahjaza.com

Clan Hidden Shadows - New York City, NY
http://www.hiddenshadowsvamp.com

House Eclipse - Washington, DC & Baltimore, MD

http://www.house-eclipse.org

Ordo Sekhemu – Texas
http://www.ordo-sekhemu.org

House Dark Haven - Savannah, GA
http://www.housedarkhaven.com

House Crimson Blade – Mississippi
http://www.housecrimsonblade.tk

House Lost Haven - Sacramento, CA
http://www.losthaven.cc

House Of Ottawa - Ottawa, Canada
http://www.houseofottawa.com

House Of The Hydra - New York City, NY
http://www.myspace.com/houseofthehydra

House Aeterno
http://www.houseaeterno.co.nr

House Of Mystic Echoes - Louisiana
http://groups.myspace.com/houseofmysticechoes

House Solaris - New Orleans, LA
http://www.myspace.com/shroudedcouncil

House Rosa
http://www.houserosa.org

The Order of Maidenfear
http://www.stonebench.us/maidenfear

House Of The Morning Star - Egypt
http://www.houseofmorningstar.tk

House Obsidian - North Carolina
http://www.houseobsidian.com

House Konatus
http://www.konatus.com

The Court Of Lazarus - A Metropolitan Vampire Society
http://www.courtoflazarus.org

The Court Of Lightning Bay - A Vampire Gathering
http://www.vampiregathering.com

TWILIGHT - A Formal Gathering Of The Vampire Community
http://www.meetup.com/twilight

Black Oaks Savannah - A Vampyre Gathering
http://www.blackoakssavannah.com

Black Trillium - A Vampyre Gathering
http://www.blacktrillium.com

Black Sunset - A Vampyre Gathering
http://groups.myspace.com/blacksunsetnoir

Endless Night Festival
http://www.endlessnight.com

Dracula's Ball - Philadelphia, PA
http://www.draculasball.com

Vampire's Masquerade Ball - Portland, OR
http://www.vampireballpdx.com

The GraveYard Press - E-Zine Publication
http://www.thegraveyardpress.com

Shadowdance Podcast
http://www.shadowdancepodcast.com

Out Of The Coffin Podcast
http://www.outofthecoffin.com

Vampire Zilchy YouTube Channel
http://www.youtube.com/user/vampirezilchy
http://www.vampirezilchy.co.nr

Vampyre Lounge Video Archive
http://www.vampyrelounge.com

Allure of the Vampire by Corvis Nocturnum

Dark Moon Press

P.O. Box 11496

Fort Wayne, Indiana 46858-1496

DarkMoon@darkmoonpress.com

www.darkmoonpress.com

Allure of the Vampire by Corvis Nocturnum

Embracing the Darkness
Understanding Dark Subcultures
By Corvis Nocturnum

The initial book of Dark Moon Press, written by author Corvis Nocturnum, which brings you an unprecedented collection of Satanists, vampires, modern primitives, dark pagans, and gothic artists, all speaking to you in their own words. These are people who have taken something most others find frightening or destructive, and woven it into amazing acts of creativity and spiritual vision.

Corvis himself is a dark artist and visionary, and so it is with the eye of a kindred spirit that he has sought these people out to share their stories with you.
$17.95 USD, 242 pages, paperback
May 2005
Cover art by Corvis Nocturnum

Cover design by Monolith Graphic

A Mirror Darkly
By Corvis Nocturnum

A collection of essays on society, philosophy and life in general written in the thought provoking way that only Corvis Nocturnum, author of the well received *Embracing the Darkness; Understanding Dark Subcultures* can, in this volume he brings you his personal collection of essays penned from years observing his fellow man. Few authors since Nietzsche or LaVey have so vehemently railed against societal, religious and governmental hypocrisies, laughable shortcomings and failings.
Sharply critical of apathetic bottom feeders to being thoughtfully introspective, Corvis forces us to look at the creature that stares back at us from the abyss.

$16.95 USD, 152 pages, paperback
May 2006

Promethean Flame
By Corvis Nocturnum

Exploring the lineage of challengers of dogmatic thinking, from the Renaissance and our modern day, *Promethean Flame* delves deep into religion, philosophy, secret societies and the arts to explain the importance that challengers of the past still have on our future.

$19.95 USD, 242 pages, paperback
October 2008

I, Lucifer Exploring the Archetype and Origins of the Devil

By Corvis Nocturnum.

I, Lucifer challengers the idea that the Devil is a real being, and proposes that he is merely an archetype that has evolved from our collective unconscious, developed and reshaped constantly from barrowed ideas and given strength by sheer numbers of believers. It explores the myths and legends of not only Satan, but Lilith, his fellow fallen angels, and the origin of Hell itself.

Covering the vast perception of Satan from his origins to our modern day depictions in literature and film, this work also studies the impact in popular culture and in the public's impression as it evolved over the decades.

$19.99 USD, 240 pages, paperback

Tentative release date May 2010

These Haunted Dreams

By Michelle Belanger

Dark, sensuous, and lyrical, the supernatural fiction of author Michelle Belanger has enchanted the readers of *Shadowdance, Necropolis,* and *Wicked Mystic* since 1991. Now, collected for the first time, enjoy the chilling and erotic tales of vampires, demon lovers, and ghostly visitations in *These Haunted Dreams*. A visionary artist sees too deeply into the secret life of one of his models. A businessman obsessed with time runs late for work and changes his life forever. A new homeowner discovers that his beloved residence is alive and has no intention of letting him leave. And many more...

Cover art by Corvis Nocturnum.

$16.95 USD, 135 pages, paperback

Allure of the Vampire by Corvis Nocturnum

Sacred Hunger
By Michelle Belanger

Author Michelle Belanger has fascinated and informed readers about the vampire in folklore, fiction, and fact since the early 90s. Now enjoy all of Michelle's major essays on this fascinating topic, collected for the first time in one volume. Find out why author Bram Stoker wrote about vampires -- and what real-life psychic vampire inspired the figure of Dracula. Learn about the history and development of the modern community of real vampires. Explore the allure of the vampire in modern culture, and meet members of the vampire underground who have made this potent archetype a fundamental part of their lives...

$16.95 USD, 164 pages, paperback

Allure of the Vampire by Corvis Nocturnum

This Trembling Flesh
By Michelle Belanger

Get your fetish fix in style. *This Trembling Flesh* features over a hundred lush and sensual images in luxurious full-color. Featuring the modeling talents of author and vocalist Michelle Belanger with numerous guests, including the vampire Don Henrie.

$34.95 USD, 138 pages, paperback

Allure of the Vampire by Corvis Nocturnum

Allure of the Vampire by Corvis Nocturnum